To Helen
with love at Christmas!
xxx
Pauline, Craig and
Alexandra

Dec. 1987

FROM THE WILD

FROM THE WILD

Portfolios of North America's Finest Wildlife Artists

Edited by Christopher Hume

INTRODUCTION BY DAVID M. LANK

PUBLISHED BY SUMMERHILL PRESS

Toronto

© Summerhill Press Ltd. 1986

Published by:
  Summerhill Press Ltd.
  Five Clarence Square
  Toronto, Ontario M5V 1H1

First published in French by:
  Éditions du Trécarré
  2973 rue Sartelon
  Ville Saint-Laurent, Quebec

Canadian Cataloguing in Publication Data
Hume, Christopher, 1951 From the wild : portfolios of North America's
finest wildlife artists

ISBN 0-920197-29-9

1. Wildlife art — Canada. 2. Wildlife art —
United States. 3. Wildlife artists — Canada.
4. Wildlife artists — United States. I. Title

N7660.H85 1986   704.9'432   C86-094085-3

Design and Production: Michael Waldin
Editor-in-Chief: Christoper Hume
Editor: Judith Drynan
Contributing Writers: Judith Drynan, Christopher Hume,
Robert Jones, David M. Lank, and Glen Warner
Colour Separation: Legg Brothers, Toronto

Color Lithograph: General Printers, Oshawa
Printed on 100 lb. Jenson Gloss, Provincial Papers

Black and White Lithograph: John Deyell Company, Lindsay
Printed on 80 lb. Byronic, Domtar Papers

Typography: Computype, Toronto

The publisher would like to thank American Cyanamid Co. and Cyanamid
Canada Inc. for the support given in the production of this book.

ISBN 0-920197-29-9

Printed and Bound in Canada

Cover Illustations:
  Front: Wood Ducks; Glen Loates, 1986.
  Back: Orca Breaching; Claudio D'Angelo, 1982.
    Silent as the Snow; Bob Kuhn, 1982.
    Red Foxes and Beech Tree; George McLean, 1977.
Page One: Terry Shortt; Secretary Bird, 1968.
Title Page: Robert Bateman; Evening Light (Detail), 1981.

Bob Kuhn: Silent as the Snow; acrylic, 24 x 36, 1982.

Glen Loates: Common Loon with Young; watercolor, 27 x 32, 1985.

Glen Loates: Common Loon with Young; watercolor, 27 x 32, 1985.

ERRATA PAGE

Page 4. Cover Illustration. Front: Wood Ducks (Detail); Glen Loates, 1986.
Page 15, col. 2, line 27: 'American Ornithology'
Page 16. Caption: John James Audubon.
Page 19, col. 2, line 24: Oceanic Birds of South America.
Page 20, col. 2, line 36: Thoreau Macdonald.
Page 46. Canada Geese; watercolor, 24 x 18, 1966.
Page 48. Bald Eagle; watercolor, 49 x 63, 1982.
Page 95. Queen Anne's Lace and American Goldfinch; acrylic, 11 x 15, 1982.
Page 127. Goldfinch Group; watercolor, 13 x 17, 1985.
Page 129. Siberian Tiger; watercolor, 7′ x 5′, 1984. © 1984 Electrolux Corporation.

Contents

Preface
— 9 —

Introduction
by David M. Lank

— 13 —

THE ARTISTS/ THE ART

List of Illustrations

— 189 —

Claudio D'Angelo: Red Fox with Grouse; oil, 20 x 34; 1986.

Preface

Fenwick Lansdowne: Common Merganser; watercolor, 32 x 24, 1976.

Sometime during the last fifteen or twenty years, wildlife art has emerged as one of the most popular art forms in North America. Thousands upon thousands of limited edition reproductions of paintings by the leading artists are bought annually. Original works are strictly a rich man's game; the big names routinely fetch between $50,000 and $100,000 a painting.

Yet animal painting is a genre in search of respectability. Within the politics of art, it occupies a hopelessly isolated position, with many official institutions, and the artistic mainstream in general, dismissing it completely. This is hardly surprising since the main concern of animal painters — the pleasant and accurate depiction of nature — is one that lies well beyond the issues that preoccupy 'serious' artists. With a few exceptions, modern art has not been deeply involved in creating the illusion of reality for well over a century. Magic realism and high realism are two examples that come to mind, but even these movements addressed themselves more to the question of perception than to objective reality.

The fact remains that, although wildlife painting provides a plus for the many people who prefer well-crafted art with recognizable imagery, it is still considered unabashedly old-fashioned and out-of-date in its outlook and methods.

Although there are historical precedents dating back thousands of years to the earliest cave paintings, it wasn't until the 1800s that wildlife art was recognized as a genre in its own right, albeit a genre with problems. Most serious has been its ambiguous relationship with popular taste. Too often, wildlife artists find themselves trapped by the demands of the public, and rather than reflect popular taste, have pandered to it. Right now in North America, the number of wildlife artists could almost equal the wildlife, and the overwhelming majority of them are busy churning out nature kitsch. Their concerns are crassly commercial; their results, sickly sentimental.

But there are kernels of genuine talent among the chaff. To deny the accomplishments of this handful of artists would be to ignore their skill and commitment. Part naturalist, part painter, the complete wildlife artist must master several disciplines. At its best, wildlife painting is an activity which requires not only knowledge, but obvious abilities and imagination. It can be done well or poorly. The latter need not concern us. The former should.

As the artists included in this book make clear, technical excellence is now almost routine. However, it is equally clear that, by itself, technical excellence is not enough. Beauty is needed. The more adventurous have renounced strict realism for approaches which are more impressionistic, holistic, and subjective. Indeed, the works of some artists, notably Lanford Monroe and George McLean, often seem more like landscapes with animals than traditional wildlife art. The most popular painters in the field, Robert Bateman and Bob Kuhn for example, take a middle course, using full landscape but placing the subject in the center of the painting. When you look at a Bateman, you are looking at a picture of an animal. Look at a Monroe, and the first thing you are likely to see is landscape. It takes a minute or two to find a living creature.

Slowly, even reluctantly, wildlife painting is evolving into a genre that can claim more than a mass audience. Perhaps in this age of postmodernism, a more sympathetic yet serious appraisal of nature art will be possible. Already a backlash has developed, but it is as one-sided in its opposition as admirers are in support.

What has become clear is that wildlife art is outgrowing it traditional boundaries. With some exceptions, the artists represented in this book do not restrict themselves to reproducing the infinite detail of hair and feathers. Although they have all specialized in wildlife, they are, first and foremost, artists. They are painters who think more about painting than about painting animals: artists who are not naturalists but who must become naturalists. The irony is that so far, the institutional support for wildlife art has come from places like museums of natural science. In Canada, for instance, many of the best-known animal painters have exhibited at one time or another at the Royal Ontario Museum. The list includes Bateman, McLean, Fenwick Lansdowne and Glen Loates. In the United States, where there is a larger and more active market, private commerical galleries dealing in wildlife art have long existed. The older generation of American wildlife artists, like Kuhn and Meltzoff, started their professional lives as illustrators, and served long apprenticeships with mass circulation journals such as Field and Stream, Argosy, True, National Geographic and Life. When the demand for illustration began to drop off in the 1960s, they made the transition to wildlife art with ease.

Like their Canadian counterparts, they prefer the big, the powerful, and the spectacular. It is not often you see a painting of a groundhog, a mole or a mouse. The perennial favorite has always been African big game, though there has been a switch to North American wildlife in recent years and nowadays the creatures of choice are more likely to be eagles, cougars, bears, moose and the like. As

Lanford Monroe: The Fox; oil, 36 x 24, 1981.

painters of wildlife, these artists are heirs to the romantic notion that nature is divine. The fact that the natural world is being destroyed at an unprecedented rate only heightens the urgency of the appeal. Many of the animals beloved by wildlife artists are threatened with imminent extinction. Indeed, for a great number of species, it is only a matter of time.

Against this backdrop, wildlife art takes on an added poignancy. It harkens back to a distant, mythical age when the world was a Garden of Eden and animals roamed at will. The fact that wildlife art has gained momentum at roughly the same time as the conservative movement is no coincidence. Awarenesss of one leads inevitably to appreciation of the other. Some artists, notably Robert Bateman and Roger Tory Peterson, are closely identified with the nature conservancy movement, while virtually all the artists contribute paintings and sketches to fund raising efforts, or participate somehow in environmental causes.

At the same time, there is a strain running through wildlife art that speaks of the human need to control, catalogue and contain. In this regard one immediately thinks of Fenwick Lansdowne, one of the pre-eminent painters of birds working anywhere in the world today. Through his series of illustrated books, he has produced as systematic an examination of North American avian life since John James Audubon, while Roger Tory Peterson's Illustrated Field Guides are an institution in themselves. With millions of books sold since they first appeared, the field guides can truly be said to have raised generations of bird watchers and artists.

How wildlife art will survive mass popularity remains to be seen. So far it seems that the good gets better, the bad gets worse. Strong collector interest has enabled the better, but less commercial artists, a chance to pursue more individual routes. Rather than turning out one animal

John Schoenherr. Double Bull; egg tempera, 28 x 40, 1980.

portrait after another, painters like McLean and Monroe are interested in depicting what they see around them. Both live in rural areas and have been increasingly involved in trying to make wildlife art more reflective of the real world by painting ordinary-looking but delightful birds, animals and environments. No charging rhinos or snarling lions — just bucolic scenes of rural America and Canada. In the familiarity of the images they produce, one senses a desire to cleanse wildlife art of its conventions, and strip it down to something more direct, simple and honest.

What makes these paintings exciting is the way they form a living record of one person's relationship with the natural world. It is no longer a matter of exalting or of cataloguing, but of looking, learning and understanding.

The most memorable examples are those that offer insight into man's role in the natural order of life on earth and how it has been irrevocably altered.

If McLean and Monroe point to the future of wildlife painting, the remaining artists embody the finest in current practice. The next few years will be interesting ones for wildlife art, which, if it is not to degenerate into commerciality and redundancy, must keep developing, evolving and growing.

Ultimately, the future of wildlife art rests with wildlife artists. On the basis of works included in this book, there is reason for optimism. The next decade could be the best yet.

Introduction

A Cave Painting of a Bull in Lascaux, France

From the dawn of civilization, man has created an artistic bond with his fellow creatures, whether by figures carved on bone, modelled in clay, or painted on the walls of caves. The interrelationship of man and animals is as old as man himself. To survive, man needed to guarantee good hunting and fishing, and art — the most primitive expression of man's awareness of self — was the chosen medium. Animals were painted with a swirling, mystical quality on the walls of limestone caves in what is now Lascaux and Altamira in France and Spain, in the virtually inaccessible overhangs of the Sierra de San Francisco in Baja, California, and the sun-scorched rocks of North Africa. Today, particularly in North America, wildlife art, the grandest mirror and interpreter of our commitment to the natural world, is more widely appreciated than at any other time in history.

Our modern approach to animal art, that animals are regarded for their own sakes and not as an adjunct to man, is one which was also held by the Romans. The eruption of Mount Vesuvius in 79 A.D. buried beautiful frescoes depicting easily recognizable birds and serpents which were lost to the

George Townley Stubbs: Horses Fighting (1788); Art Gallery of Ontario, Toronto.

However, Josef Wolf, whose portrait of a falcon for Schlegel's *Traité du Fauconnerie* in 1844 is considered a masterpiece, took exception to the artistry of painting dead animals, complaining: "If you paint a dead linnet or a red poll, it is admissable to the Royal Academy. If you paint it alive, it is a transcript of an object of Natural History, unfit for exhibition." He understood that it requires far greater observation and technical skill to capture the essence of a living, moving, tension-filled animal than to copy an inanimate or formerly animate object.

Pets have also figured prominently in the history of animal arts. Whether as diversions in Carpaccio's "Two Courtesans" from the early Italian Renaissance, or as a prop in Gerard ter Borch's "Visit of the Suitor" from 1658, pets have appeared as social symbols in thousands of paintings down through the centuries and in countless cultures. There is also a huge body of work devoted to portraits of the pets themselves. Sir Edwin Landseer, Queen Victoria's favorite painter, was a great dog portraiturist, as was George Stubbs, perhaps better known for his horse paintings.

Domesticated animals have long been considered subjects worthy of serious artistic endeavor. Paulus Potter and Aelbert Cuyp, the great Dutch masters, were famous for their life-sized compositions of cattle and sheep. In our own time, some of the finest work of the late English artist Charles Tunnicliffe, was devoted to pigs, sheep, cows and horses — especially the wonderfully dignified Clydesdales. Horses were also painted by such greats as John Charles Maggs during the heyday of the stage coaches in England.

There has also been a significant tradition of sporting art. During the 19th century, artists such as John Frederick Herring Sr. and Ben Marshall painted the winners of horse races, while George Wright captured the fox hunt in all its yelping, red-coated confusion, pouring over hedgerows and streams in the most romanticized of English countrysides. There was even a fashionable school of angling painting, which littered the banks of English and American streams with expiring corpses of salmon, trout and pike. In a style similar to much of today's work, there tended to be a preoccupation with detail, which demanded that every scale be faithfully shown.

From the 15th century to the early 19th century, animal art

world until discovered 1700 years later, just at the time Europeans had begun to appreciate animals in their own right. In the interim, serious artists regarded animals only in their relationship to humans. The Bible said that man should have dominion over every living thing that moved upon the earth, and this 'dominion' was taken seriously. Animals, when they were portrayed at all, tended to be depicted in the service of man.

In the 14th and 15th centuries, many noblemen commissioned sumptuously illustrated manuscript versions of Gaston Phoebus' *The Book of Hunting* to bolster their manly image. These depictions of the hunt provide great scope for close observation of the various European species, some of which, sadly, have disappeared since the Middle Ages. The hunt includes the kill, and few painters have matched Jean-Baptiste Chardin (1699 — 1779) for accuracy in depicting death. In one of his paintings, a hare, suspended by a foot over the kitchen counter, contrasts wonderfully with the glowing, burnished copper of the cauldron. The rabbit's fur is matted and dishevelled, the eyes are sunken, and the tension in the backbone is broken, allowing the legs to stretch and hang at angles that would be impossible if the animal were still alive.

received a significant thrust from the development of illustrations in books documenting man's emerging understanding of the natural world, even though art was sacrificed to scientific draftsmanship. The subjects were usually done in strict profile, with, as Josef Wolf grumbled about a fellow artist, every mistake of the bird-stuffer faithfully copied. However, with growing knowledge of nature, and the interest in the species continually being discovered through world exploration, animal art in books slowly developed. Thomas Bewick of Newcastle-upon-Tyne made an incredible contribution between the late 1700s and 1828. As the rediscoverer of the lost art of wood engraving, as opposed to wood-cutting, he brought a technical innovation that would dominate the illustration of books for the next seventy-five years: as the first English artist to draw and paint directly from live birds and mammals, he was able to combine an understanding of living beings with a technical and artistic mastery.

John Gould was important in the history of animal art, even though he scarcely ever completed a painting himself. Instead, he classified and arranged skins which came to his "bird factory" from all over the world, which were then painted by such famous artists as Edward Lear and John Keulemans, for

Thomas Bewick: Hare Coursing; Bewick Wood Engravings, Victoria and Albert Museum, London.

what became a series of forty-three imperial portfolios. In the 3,159 hand-colored plates, the birds and mammals were done in realistic if somewhat static poses against very decorative backgrounds, and the consistency of excellence in so large a work is unparalled in wildlife art. Josef Wolf, of the slightly acerbic tongue, was by far the best-known of Gould's artists. Landseer stated that he was "without exception the best all-round animal painter that ever lived" and Archibald Thorburn, who was to dominate English animal painting in the early decades of the 20th century, called his art "faultless." Looking beyond the somewhat formal plates he did for Gould, the 'sketches' he did for the London Zoological Society prove that he was just as much at home with fur as with feather. He could capture the alertness in the ears of a fox as easily as he could portray the stop-start feeding movements of yellow-billed storks. By the middle of the 19th century he had brought art and science together, and his plates, along with those of his wonderously prolific pupil John Keulemans, exemplify the Golden Age of Natural History art as an adjunct to the growing interest in scientific knowledge.

Wildlife art took a giant step forward with the emergence of the American artist, John James Audubon. The best bird painter in the early 1800s was acknowledged to be an expatriate Scottish poet named Alexander Wilson, who was in North America looking not only for new species of birds, but for subscribers to his ambitious and expensive 'American Anthology.' In Henderson, Kentucky, he happened into a frontier store belonging to Audubon, and had just convinced him to sign up for the series, when Audubon's partner, Fernand Rozier, fortuitously interrupted the proceedings and pointed out that Audubon's own drawings and paintings far surpassed anything that Wilson had done. Audubon determined there and then to publish his own collection. The course of animal art was changed forever when he displayed his paintings in Edinburgh in 1827. Not only were his birds ornithologically correct, they were also life-size — from the largest whooping crane to the smallest hummingbird — and due to his skill as an artist, as well as his method of wiring freshly killed specimens onto a grid for models, depicted as they would look in life. The thousands of miles he had travelled through the wilderness

James Audubon: Mockingbird.

magnificent folios of the birds and animals from specific countries or continents. Tens of thousands of hand-colored plates, sometimes numbering in the millions of copies, were lithographed by, or after, some of the finest wildlife artists of all time.

During the latter decades of the 19th century there was a wonderful light emanating from the Northern European countries. In Germany, William Kuhnert was establishing his world reputation as a big-game painter, while in Sweden, Bruno Liljefors was redefining whole artistic concepts so brilliantly that today his paintings are considered national treasures. He always understood that the way to capture an animal's essence was not through slavish attention to every detail, but by an accurate depiction of form and posture, bulk and attitude, and above all, through the play of light and atmosphere inherent in a living situation. His impact on the development of animal art in Europe cannot be overstated.

The same can be said of Switerland's Léo-Paul Robert, a towering genius whose ease with perspective allowed his birds to achieve a natural quality unsurpassed even by Liljefors. He knew that the mind would fill in what the eye could not see, and was perfectly comfortable in having a bird's tail or wing extend beyond the limits of the canvas. His understanding of color and featheration produced the effect of detail where, indeed, only broad brushstrokes existed. More that anyone, he could infuse the eye of a bird with an almost frightening sense of life. Largely unknown outside of Switzerland today, Robert was hailed in the late 18th and early 19th centuries as the greatest painter in Europe.

had also given him an unparalleled exposure to birds and animals in their living environments, and, of all the aspects of Audubon's art, his placing of birds in their natural habitat would have the most profound impact. Although this approach has been considered the norm ever since, it was the first time in published animal art that birds had been placed in their proper ecological settings.

Audubon raised the level of natural history illustration to that of art, and once the ground had been broken, others followed rapidly. The new artists were able to use the artistic and technological breakthroughs of the times to satisfy the public's demand for outstanding art. Monographs on virtually every known family of bird were produced, as well as

Carl Rungius stands just one step behind these two great wildlife artists. His paintings of the larger North American mammals rank among the great monuments of animal art. Born in Germany in 1869, he was a consumate painter of the outdoors, and during his career was considered the master. He had a passion for big game, and his portraits and reproductions of moose, elk, bighorn sheep and grizzly bear, made the West a palpaple reality for thousands of armchair travellers and art lovers. His classical training was evident in his early career when all colors were skillfully blended in the traditional manner, but in later years he freed himself from this academic style, and turned to broad bold

Leo Robert: Corneille Noire; Les Oiseaux de Chez Nous.

areas of pure color lavished on the canvasses with wide strokes. From a proper distance, the colors seem to overlap and coalesce, igniting the scene with radiant sunlight or cooling it with somber shadow. Modern painters of both the photographic and impressionistic schools point to Rungius as an inspiration. His own inspiration was the wilderness, the same deep influence that has shaped and colored all North American animal art since the first primitive watercolors painted by John White in the Roanoke Colony, Virginia, between 1548 and 1590.

The wilderness influenced animal painting from earliest times. The arrival of the Europeans brought artists to document the wildlife, artists such as Peter Paillou and Sydney Parkinson who painted the birds and animals collected by Sir Joseph Banks during his voyage to Newfoundland and Labrador in 1766. Parkinson placed his birds in imaginative poses in more or less appropriate ecological settings, raising scientific portraiture to the highest level then known. Audubon himself travelled up through Cape Breton Island and along the Labrador coast, a voyage which resulted in twenty-three finished paintings for the double elephant folio *Birds of America*. Despite his delight in discovering the new birds which added such interest to "the wonderful dreariness" of the land, he was moved to write in his Labrador Journal of

1833: "Seldom in my life have I left a country with as little regret as I do this."

Robert Hood, one of Canada's first wildlife artists and a midshipman with Sir John Franklin, never got the chance to leave. In 1821, he was, according to his tombstone, "assassinated by an Iroquois, thus terminating at the age of four-and-twenty a short but brilliant career." Hood's watercolors of the birds and animals from the area of Cumberland House and Fort Enterprise were among the first, and in some cases the very first paintings of western species. They remained lost for 150 years.

The Great Plains offered another seemingly inexhaustible resource; the buffalo. These mighty animals, which once roamed the plains in their millions before being almost wiped out by hunters, were inextricably tied up with the art of Canada's first great indigenous painter of the West, Frederick Arthur Verner. Born in Halton County, Ontario in 1836, Verner was active when the fur trade was coming to an end, and Indians were subjugated by treaties they signed but could not understand. American greats such as Charles Marion Russell fully appreciated Verner's talents on a professional level, while the newspaper critics of a Romantic Age rhapsodized that his

Carl Rungius: Kodiak Bear; Art Gallery of Ontario, Toronto.

Frederick Verner: Buffalo; McCord Museum, McGill University, Montreal.

In notebooks which still exist, Seton made many black-and-white sketches of species in flight, specifically to aid in instantaneous recognition. Here, unmistakably, is the genesis of the field guide. The 'realism' inherent in the modern field guide has heavily influenced many of today's painters who adhere to an almost photographic style, the "I-can-see-every-feather" school, so it is ironic that the original purpose of the field guide was to downplay detail, and concentrate on pattern and silhouette. Even a superficial comparison between the original Peterson field guide of 1934 and the latest edition will prove the point: yesterday's form has become today's detail.

However, Peterson, through his field guide 'bibles', has almost single-handedly revolutionized the relationship of man and animals by allowing field identification to come to the layman. Unlike the 19th century-style museum men (of whom Josef Wolf complained: "Some ornithologists don't know nature — don't know a bird when they see it flying. A specimen must be well-dried before they recognize it.") today's artists are experienced field observers. As a result, we not only have better science, but better art.

The role of books and magazines in the development of American animal art is too often and too quickly dismissed under the false assumption that all the thousands of pictures in them were mere illustration. There is no question that, from the early 1930s right through to the 1950s, the greatest patron of animal art was the publishing industry, which commissioned the works of young painters like Roger Tory Peterson, George Miksch Sutton, and Don Eckleberry. In the 1920s and 1930s, virtually every major book and magazine sought the works of Louis Agassiz Fuertes, who had an uncanny knack of catching his birds and mammals in the act of looking natural. It was his influence rather than specific pictures, however, which had the greatest impact on other artists whose careers overlapped or followed his. Two tower above the rest in those early years: Major Allan Brooks and Francis Lee Jaques, both largely forgotten by the public, but remembered and emulated by artists. Fifty years ago, they were the acknowledged leaders, and without first looking at their contributions, the artistic base for today's outpouring of animal art cannot be fully appreciated.

work was "more than a mere reproduction of the landscape — it is a poem!" In 1926, the Toronto Globe stated that his scenes of buffalo life on the plains were "a class of subject where he stands alone and unrivalled." Inevitably his subject matter brought him into contact with the civilizations of the Indians, and he became a documentarist of their rapidly vanishing lifestyles.

At the turn of the century, the unquestioned master of animal portraiture was the Canadian Ernest Thompson Seton, who later, as an American, became famous as the co-founder of the Boy Scouts of America. It would seem that Seton never considered his work to have lasting value, as he never wasted hard-earned cash on paints which would endure. Today, much of his finest work is in lamentable shape, but more than enough has been saved by museums such as the Seton Museum in Cimmaron to document his genius. It was in the area of the field guide, however, that Seton made a contribution that has been overlooked by many and de-emphasized by many more. Without doubt, the concept of the field guide, which has been carried to its highest level by Roger Tory Peterson, has changed for all time the way man sees nature. But Peterson openly acknowledges that his inspiration came from two little pages containing line drawings of different kinds of ducks in Seton's classic outdoor book for boys from 1903, *Two Little Savages*.

Allan Brooks: Barn Swallow, Cliff Swallow & Purple Martin (1934); Bird Portraits in Color, University of Minnesota Press, 1934.

extreme, or scaly coats of mail at the other. Brooks gives the impression that the feathers could be ruffled, only to have them fall back into place again to serve the living bird. He was blessed with ornithological genius from his earliest days, and became one of the finest field naturalists in North America during his long life. His knowledge was legendary and earned him the nickname, the Pope of ornithology.

Perhaps the most fascinating book for students of bird art is *The Birds of Minnesota*, published in 1932 and containing a posthumous plate by Fuertes, elegant early examples by George Miksch Sutton, several by Walter A. Weber, and the first works of John Breckenridge. The principal artist was Brooks, about whom the author, Thomas S. Roberts wrote: " . . . it may be stated that Major Allan Brooks is a Canadian . . . and that he is generally considered to be the leading portrayer of birds and mammals in North America." It was this book which confirmed the superior work of Francis Lee Jaques as well, who, Brooks remarked, "stands alone in America in making a bird picture."

In 1936, Jaques' reputation for book illustration and museum dioramas, especially in Minnesota and New York, made him the logical choice to supply the scientifically and artistically stunning plates for Robert Cushman Murphy's Oceanic Books of South America, one of the most significant books of the century. Jaques loved the horizon, whether very high or very low. It allowed him a wonderful flexibility of design, with the birds and mammals being naturally integrated with their accompanying flowers, mountains, cliffs, canyons, breakers, streams and lakes. Nothing was static. His view of the Peruvian Blue-Footed Boobies is from below; the birds in their mating dance contrast against the dome of the blue sky, while high overhead floats a condor on wings made small by distance. In his works, the brush paints less than the mind sees, and the result raises Jaques' compositions to levels that soar above mere illustrations of scientific accuracy.

Jaques was perhaps the best practitioner of black-and-white sketches, another side of art in North America which is far too often overlooked. Unfortunately, the poor quality of paper during his peak years precluded a level of printing which did justice to his work. *The Singing Wilderness*, *Listening Point*, and scores of other books, contain illustrations that are among the best of the genre. Henry B. Kane's work for *Cache Lake Country*, and Terry Shortt's for *The Last of the Curlews*, *Arctic*

Born in 1869 in England, but a true son of the Canadian west, Allan Brooks inherited the mantel of Fuertes, his younger friend and contemporary, whose brilliant career was prematurely ended by a tragic traffic accident. Brooks painted endlessly for the National Geographic Magazine, but the final form of the pictures was largely determined by the editors. This lack of freedom was further hampered by the less than perfect color and register of the printing process, and, of course, the severe reduction in size diminished the chance for serious artistic appraisal. However, the overall compositions stand on their own as superior works of landscape art.

His greatest strength was his "feel" for feathers and his uncanny ability to capture their physical structure, not just in coloration, but in function. Texturally, far too many artists with obsessive attention to detail render feathers as hair at one

Birds, and *Birds of Ontario* deserve far greater recognition, as does the black-and-white material that Roger Tory Peterson supplied for *Wild America* and other books. This 'minor' art form draws on a tradition dating back to Albrecht Durer in the early 16th century, Thomas Bewick in the late 18th and early 19th centuries, and Charles Tunnicliffe in our own.

Another etcher who must be mentioned is Ogden Pleissner, perhaps the most accomplished and versatile painter since Winslow Homer. In the 1940s, he experimented brilliantly with drypoint in scenes of bird shooting and salmon fishing. He had a huge influence on later artists, but his importance also lay in the commercial exploitation of the limited edition art print, so much a feature of today's art world. Pleissner's first was called "Atlantic Salmon Fishing" and was limited to 300 copies when published in 1939. From then until his death in 1984, he published another 30 hunting and fishing subjects with never more than 400 copies; a far cry from editions these days 'limited' to 950 copies, plus the overrun of the artist's and publisher's proofs.

In fact, painting specifically for the print market has become the dominant activity of many artists, whose output is too often determined by what is commercial instead of what is artistic. Also, North American buyers tend to be species oriented, and as a result, a low quality painting of a bluejay with every feather frozen in photographic detail will often outsell the finest portrait of a snake. It is no coincidence that the snake plates of Mark Catesby done back in 1731, which rank among the most beautiful works of animal painting of all time, are shunned today.

However, there is also genius abroad in American wildlife painting today. Robert Verity Clemm's portraits of shorebirds in the 1967 edition of *Shorebirds of North America*, in some cases approaches the artistry of Liljefors. Bob Kuhn's paintings of African and North American game consistently demonstrate how unimportant detail is in the hands of a master who can capture mass and volume and atmosphere. No one can paint the lope of a big cat better than Kuhn who has inherited the brilliance of Rungius and Kuhnert. John Schoenherr, with his striking patterns of massive rock and sheets of gliding waters contrasting with brilliant sunlight and deep shadow, inherits Jaques' title of the superlative "picture maker." Stanley Meltzoff has created an approach to underwater painting that has revolutionized the genre by showing fish scales as mirrors of their environment, so unlike the practice of painting fish as seen in sunlight, and then placing them back in the water for an 'underwater' painting. Lanford Monroe, one of the truly superior technical landscape artists, brings a sense of discipline and training to her paintings where the settings, not the animals or birds, dominate the scene. Influences have come from other countries. Raymond Ching has brought to the American art scene a definition of super-realism that few artists can understand let alone emulate. Germany's Manfred Schatz, since his Pack of Wolves artistically overwhelmed North American audiences at the 1975 "Animals in Art" exhibition at the Royal Ontario Museum in Toronto, has liberated a whole school of painters from their obsession with detail. With this freedom has also come a belated appreciation for the works of Bob Lougheed, John Clymer and other western artists.

All the styles are different. There is no single right way to paint and excellence has many homes. But all the painters share a common concern; a caring for the preservation of today's threatened environment which has replaced the feeling of inexhaustibility of the wild that permeated the paintings of a century ago. Since then, times have changed, and the incredible number of animals and birds has been sorely diminished. Nevertheless, there are few places in the world where the wonder of nature is so much in evidence as it is in North America. Often, in the confusion of modern life, we feel the need to establish our place in the natural scheme of things, to reestablish our bonds with the spirit of the wilderness. The wildlife artist is our link with that spirit. Contemporary artists consciously or unconsciously draw on a spiritual inheritance voiced by the Canadian painter Thoreau Monroe, who, back in the 1930s claimed that his work was "... not that of a naturalist, not an artist, just that of a fond observer." No greater compliment could be paid to wildlife artists and their legacy.

ROBERT BATEMAN

Nesting Geese; acrylic, 36 x 48; 1978.

Grey Squirrel; acrylic, 16 x 24, 1981.

Robert Bateman is, by any account, the most successful wildlife artist in the world today. He has succeeded in transforming a highly specialized genre into a popular art form, and more than any other individual, is responsible for the recent upsurge of interest in contemporary animal painting. His meticulously rendered portraits of birds and animals from around the world are sought by collectors everywhere. Photo-mechanical reproductions of his works are snapped up by the tens of thousands, and his first book, *The Art of Robert Bateman* published in 1981, sold over 165,000 copies: an achievement unsurpassed by any other art book in Canadian publishing. Beyond being a painter and a naturalist, he is a phenomenon.

Yet the soft-spoken but fiercely determined Bateman has always been uncomfortable with his own fame. He regards success not only in terms of recognition from the public, but from his peers as well. "In a way, I consider the art community my world and the people in it part of my family." So the criticisms he sometimes receives from members of the 'serious' art community, that his paintings are more commercial than esthetic, keep him from getting

Sheer Drop — Mountain Goats; oil, 48 x 36, 1980.

taught art and geography for twenty years in the high schools of Toronto and Burlington, sixty kilometers east. Although he enjoyed teaching, he was never quite at home in the classroom. "I always felt like an amateur," he recalls. "I never sought promotions or anything. I threw myself into teaching, but always with the sense that I had chosen it because it would give me plenty of time to paint." In the end, it didn't give him time enough.

Bateman traces his love of nature back to his childhood. Growing up in a house located beside a large ravine, the fair-haired boy had many opportunites to study the natural world first-hand. When he was eight, his parents bought a cottage in Haliburton, a popular Ontario vacation area on James Bay, which allowed him to pursue his interest even more intensely. He began drawing birds and animals, and was an avid naturalist by the time he was twelve. He joined the Royal Ontario Museum's Junior Field Naturalists Club and, as a teenager, spent countless hours sketching and painting in the museum. "The people at the ROM were earthy and woodsy, yet extremely knowledgeable and intellectual. They reinforced all my role models."

He studied all the while, and after graduating from the Ontario College of Art, set out to be what he calls a "Group of Seven artist." Like his hero Tom Thomson, one of Canada's most gifted landscape painters, he would go to Northern Ontario's Algonquin Park to canoe and sketch. "I always made it a point of honor to finish all my work in the field," he smiles.

Bateman next moved on to abstract art with idols like Mark Rothko, Franz Kline and Clifford Still. The big change to realism came in 1963, when he visited the Albright Knox Gallery in Buffalo, N.Y. and saw an exhibition of paintings by the beloved American artist Andrew Wyeth. "I realized that here was a great painter who was also a great wildlife artist: that the two things could go together." He had always sketched flowers and animals, but hadn't taken this seriously as art. Now it dawned on the developing artist that realism was as

smug about his talents and abilities. However, he strongly rejects the concept that "there must be something wrong with a painting if the public likes it" and if he is occasionally accused of painting for popularity, he must also get credit for succeeding without compromising his own artistic principles.

Ironically, this world-renowned painter didn't become a full-time artist until 1975 when he was forty-four years old. Born in 1931 and raised in Toronto's affluent north end, he

Morning on the Flats — Bison; acrylic, 12 x 24, 1982.

viable as abstract, and that nature was as good a subject as any. By 1965, he was well into painting wildlife, but he never forgot the lessons he learned from abstract art. He points to his canvas Sheer Drop as an example of the influence of Clifford Still. "Still paints in slashes and blobs, and I'd been searching for a way to adapt that approach. Then, while I was driving through the Rocky Mountains one time, it occured to me that the mountains' jagged outlines could be my realistic slashes, and all I needed were some real-life blobs." These turned out to be the real-life mountain goats.

Bateman's unparallelled popularity seems to be based on his ability to use a painting to tell a story, and in doing so, involve the viewer. For the most part, he avoids sentimentality, he has too much respect for wildlife to trivialize it, and his travels all over the world to record different species in their natural habitat have given his paintings a definite ring of authenticity. His appeal, however, ultimately transcends the accomplishments of a naturalist or a story teller. Bateman's major artistic insight has been to place the depicted bird or animal back into a natural context, into a total landscape which includes many other elements. His artistic skill lies in making us see things which are not actually there. Some people are convinced, for example, that in the interests of realism, Bateman paints every blade of grass. Far from it. Visually, as well as in emotional terms, he gives us just enough to let us believe in the reality, but leaves plenty of room for the imagination. There is space on his canvasses not only for the wildlife, but for the viewer as well. It is this, more than anything, which forms the basis of his ability to communicate.

Bateman is also an unusually active and generous advocate of the conservation movement. Until 1986, when he and his family moved to a house on Saltspring Island on the northwest coast of British Columbia, Bateman lived near the Bruce Trail and was a member of several commissions dedicated to the preservation of this 700 kilometer hiking trail which runs the length of the Niagara Escarpment in southern Ontario. He still contributes works of art to the Niagara Escarpment Commission, as he does to other conservation groups, to help raise money. It is estimated that he has donated more than a million dollars worth of his works to help environmental causes. He has received numerous awards for his work with both international and Canadian environmental groups, and is an Officer in the Order of Canada.

Now, midway through his fifties, Bateman is an artist whose future seems secure. The difficulty will be to match and exceed the standards he has set for himself, while dealing with the demands success is making on his time and work. Maintaining his output of ten to twelve major paintings a year is tougher than ever, for underneath his calm demeanor is a man who thrives on constant activity, and he continues to travel the globe like a man possessed. There are those who feel that the paintings of the early 1980s are not as strong as his earlier works, and, indeed, some pieces are better than others. Where Bateman has improved is in his handling of paint. His works have a certain looseness now, a freedom, which comes from experience and confidence. More than ever, if there is a conflict between art and nature, art wins.

The success of Bateman's second book, *The World of Robert Bateman,* which to date has sold close to 100,000 copies, confirms his undiminished popularity and the fact that he is still the most widely sought-after artist in the genre. His works themselves form a record of one man's love affair with the natural world.

CLAUDIO D'ANGELO

Ring-Billed Gulls — Study; oil, 12 x 16, 1983.

For ten days in early October 1981, the most important wildlife art exhibit ever held in Toronto was taking place. The 130-odd pieces of art from around the world were to be auctioned at a fund-raising gala under the patronage of H.R.H. The Duke of Edinburgh, president of the World Wildlife Fund.

Many of the more than one hundred artists were household names in their native lands. Such greats as Axel Amuchastegui from Argentina, Leigh Voigt of South Africa, Bob Kuhn of the United States, Manfred Schatz of West Germany, and Sir Peter Scott of England exhibited important works. Canada proudly offered world class art by George McLean, Robert Bateman, Terry Shortt, Fenwick Lansdowne and the incomparable sculptor, Robert Phinney. To the experts, the quality of these artists' works came as no surprise. It was the outstanding quality of a significant number of "unknowns" that brought muttered disbelief, and none was was more remarkable than a young Montrealer, Claudio D'Angelo.

The start of Claudio D'Angelo's career could not have been more prosaic. Lured by the glamour of the judges — Saturday Evening Post cover names — the aspiring young artist copied a sketch in a magazine advertisment and sent it off expectantly to a correspondence art course in Connecticut. His rendition of the drawing definitely proved, according to the form letter reply, that he had great promise. All that was needed was a cheque. "All of the big-name artists must have been away," D'Angelo remembers today. "Artists I had never heard of were correcting my assignments and sending them back to me. I took their criticisms to heart, and kept at it. In any event, those people really did teach me to draw."

More accurately, they helped hone the natural ability that had been evident since childhood when he roamed the woods in his native Laval sketching his first encounters with nature. He also found inspiration in the various artists that worked for National Geographic magazine, especially Louis Agassiz Fuertes.

Further study led to a commercial art degree and a job with an advertising agency. Ironically, it was one of the agency's corporate clients that gave D'Angelo the opportunity to break into wildlife art by commissioning

Summer Resident — Wood Thrush; oil, 15 x 24, 1983.

Musk Oxen; oil, 24 x 36, 1982.

him to do a series of nine paintings. These forced D'Angelo to tackle a broad range of species, and gave him the opportunity to experiment with style and layout. The comparison of two of the paintings, the Huskies and the Musk Oxen, offers insights into his technique.

The chiseled detail of the huskies differs remarkably in style to the almost impressionistic lines and muted tones of the musk oxen. In the former, the clear Arctic sun brings a crispness to the smallest detail and even to the mountains in the background. In the musk ox painting, the swirling snow screens out the detail in the long shaggy fur and completely masks the hooves. The paintings are virtually devoid of vegetation, which forces D'Angelo to concentrate on the different textures of fur, stone and ice, vividly emphasizing the rugged endurance of the animals. But not only has D'Angelo paid great attention to the anatomical features of the animals and the various environmental elements, he has also added that most elusive ingredient: the atmosphere. The wind blowing the fur of the musk oxen is so forceful we can almost feel it, and the threatening storm clouds he builds up suggest the unseen currents that drive ice into ridges as obstacles for the huskies. He has even hinted at the high latitude through the use of long shadows in the bright sunlight.

The Blue Whale and the Orca are perhaps his most popular works to date, largely because they demonstrate his uncanny feel for the water. Like no other artist except Stanley Meltzoff, D'Angelo has been able to overcome the artistic problems posed by the unusual lighting situations underwater. The reflective and refractive properties of underwater optics is something very few artists understand or have been able to depict on canvas. The Blue Whale is an example of D'Angelo's skill in this field. The success of this painting goes beyond mere technique, for it also captures the indescribable serenity of the largest creature on earth as it begins an unhurried underwater dive. The body is wonderfully streamlined, its bulk compressed by the surrounding waterpressure into a shape envied by boat designers.

The differing artistic problems posed by an underwater scene are also more difficult than those faced in a conventional landscape. First of all, there is no horizon. On land, objects diminish in size as they get further away, but water's inherent qualities cause details to blur quickly and then disappear as objects move away. This means that, even in relatively clear water, the foreground must be much more sharply defined than the immediate background. So it is in D'Angelo's whale; the tip of the snout is detailed, the flukes are blurred. Secondly, except in very shallow and crystal water, sunlight is never direct. Some of it is reflected off the surface, refracted and filtered by the water itself. As color is, after all, a perceived combination of pigment and light, the hues seen underwater in natural light are not nearly as varied as those seen on land. The filtering action of the molecules, and the interference of suspended materials such as plankton, cause the visible spectrum to be reduced, and only certain colors can penetrate. Blues predominate in the upper levels, giving way rapidly to darker tones until no color remains at all. To achieve a sense of realism, therefore, requires careful handling of both the water and whale. To paint a fish or whale as seen on land, and then place it in a watery setting may be the favored approach of some

Still Hunter — Great Grey Owl; oil, 40 x 30, 1985.

artists, but it produces a total distortion. In reality, the surface of a fish's scales, and to a lesser degree its skin, tend to reflect the surrounding environment. The silver of a salmon as seen on a bank is the same silver that reflects the water in which swims. What is obvious on land, however, becomes frustratingly concealed underwater. So it is with the blue whale. The 'color' is really a pattern cast by the

Blue Whale; oil, 24 x 36, 1982.

filtered and refracted sunlight onto the pigment and reflection capacity of the mammal's skin, and D'Angelo conveys these patterns convincingly.

In the painting of the breaching orca, D'Angelo has captured the magic moment when the whale is suspended in the elements of both land and water. The largest and most intelligent member of the dolphin family hurtles from the depths of a British Columbia fjord with an explosion of foam and water droplets into the misty beginnings of another day. After studying the picture intently, the renowned west coast cetologist, Ronn Storro-Patterson, shook his head in disbelief. "I've never seen anyone impart such a sense of power. The orca is breaching as you'd see it in the sea, not as it would in an aquarium with a fat mullet for a reward."

Although not as well-known as some of the other artists in the wildlife field, young D'Angelo has a promising furture. His inclusion in the World Wildlife Fund auction catalogue has alreadybrought him attention from the international wildlife art community.

As good as his work is, D'Angelo recognizes his own limitations. "I've got to get out into the field more and build up a store of first hand impressions," he says. "And when I watch George McLean use the same palette of colors to create a mountain lion and a waterfall, I can only be grateful for the hints he has given me."

BOB KUHN

Three Dudes; acrylic, 18 x 36, 1980.

"Animal painting," says Bob Kuhn, "is a special calling." This is certainly true in his case. Not only does he have a reputation as one of the toughest and most uncompromising artists in the field, he is, in the judgment of many critics and collectors, the best animal painter alive today.

Kuhn can trace his calling back to early childhood. He was born in Buffalo, N.Y. in 1920, and was often taken by his father and grandfather to "a sorry little zoo" there. It may not have been much of a place, but it was enough to get young Bob started on his life-long fascination with the animal kingdom. "That handful of moth-eaten specimens caused me to flip on sight," he recalled in his 1973 book *The Animal Art of Bob Kuhn*. "The preoccupation was there when I made my first scribbles at age five or six and it's still there now." After studies at Pratt Institute in Brooklyn, Kuhn began working as a commercial artist. From the outset, his specialty was animals. In the twenty-five years he worked as a professional illustrator, he contributed to most of the popular men's magazines including Field and Stream, Argosy, True, and Outdoor Life. During the 1960s, the illustration market started to

Mouser; acrylic, 22 x 24, 1986.

loves to depict the big cats lounging and sleeping, he is primarily a painter of movement. "The problem of approximating . . . animals in motion is one that continues to plague me," he says in his book. "The flow of motion is almost impossible to reduce to two dimensions, even though you have selected the perfect instant in the endless realignment of parts."

Even more important than movement is gesture, which Kuhn calls "a vital consideration when painting anything animate." Often, he explains, a picture will begin with a gesture. "My way of doodling is to make endless arrangements of animal shapes on bond paper that I keep by my place at the kitchen table. Much of the stuff is junk, and I systematically toss it in the basket. But when a really good arrangement . . . or gesture . . . surfaces, I take it very seriously. By building on that pleasing gesture, however simple, I can very often press on to a more complete picture idea, and from that develop a viable painting."

The final and most important consideration, Kuhn believes, is the animal's character. "Capturing character is really at the heart of this pursuit. Character is comprised of both appearance and behavior. Predators move with the confidence born of a lifestyle largely unaffected by fear. The prey animals are a much more fidgety bunch, for the obvious reason that they must be forever ready to perceive danger and react. Non-predators of great power, such as the elephant, rhinoceros and buffalo, carry themselves with the confidence that their size and strength warrant." Although Kuhn got his start drawing zoo animals, he insists that even the most well-kept animals in captivity are not the same as those in the wild, since they are far less aggressive and have less well-developed muscles.

In spite of his love of African animals, Kuhn has switched his emphasis lately to North American wildlife. "Ten percent of what I do now is African, and the rest is North American." The reason is simple: this is what the public

decline and painting began to occupy more and more of his time. By 1975, he decided he was ready to make the switch and become a full-time wildlife artist. "The kids were out of college and I had established that I could make a living selling paintings." The time was ripe for a new career.

For the next five years Kuhn concentrated on painting African big game, reflecting an affectionate relationship with the continent he has visited nine times so far. He points out that he has spent more than a year there in total, and much of that time has been devoted to observing his favorite creature — the lion. To date, he has completed "about forty" lion paintings and more will undoubtedly follow. "I paint mainly big game," he says, including elephants and water buffalo among his other preferred animals, "and a lot of active predation stuff." This means animals hunting and killing other animals, for although he

Two Bulls; acrylic, 24 x 36, 1975.

wants. There is an increasing awareness of the balance of nature on this continent, he feels, and with awareness comes interest. The change is one Kuhn has accomplished with apparent ease. His dramatic, sometimes spine-tingling portraits of grizzly bears and mountain goats rank among his most successful pieces, although painting into the public demand has its problems. "Sometimes I can't think of what to do next," he says. "After all, how many moose can you paint in a year?" However, since he is doing more painting now than ever before, these problems have not proved insurmountable. "Up to the '80s, I finished about fifteen works annually, but now I'm painting lots of little pieces so my output has increased to between twenty-five and twenty-eight paintings a year."

Early Snow on Good Hill; acrylic, 22 x 24, 1965.

Although he has never been concerned with achieving microscopic accuracy, Kuhn spends as much time as possible in the field to get first-hand knowledge and experience of animals in their natural habitat. In that respect he resembles the people who buy his paintings; most of whom, he claims, are hunters. The difference is that Kuhn travels with a sketchpad rather than a gun. A consumate draftsman, he has honed his skills through years of practice, and although he does some of his painting out of doors, he prefers the directness of drawing. He is also able to get some accurate and useful sketches while watching wildlife programs on television. Many offer sights which could take months of field work to see. For example, in all his time observing African big game, Kuhn has never actually seen one animal kill another, but he can catch remarkable footage of this on television. He was particularly interested in the National Geographic special which showed a tiger stalking and killing its prey, and madly made sketches throughout the program for future reference. All drawings are filed according to species in large folders that can be pulled out when needed. The files have grown thick with the passage of time: with the accumulated sketches of a life spent observing and recording. There are even a few faded scribblings which date back to early days at the Buffalo Zoo.

Kuhn also uses slides as reference material, which he either takes himself or buys from professional photographers. If he can't find what he needs among his thousands of transparencies, he turns to his library of wildlife books, a nearby zoo, or the American Museum of Natural History in New York.

For the last thirty-five years, Kuhn has lived in rural Connecticut on the edge of a 125-acre nature reserve, giving him a good deal of contact with local wildlife. "We've got all kinds of animals around here, including coyotes and a helluva lot of deer." Neighbors call him up when they find a carcass, and even if he comes across something as small as a mouse, he will often sketch it. As he

King of the Road; acrylic, 20 x 40, 1982.

says: "Any species which has survived until today is either tough, adaptable or lucky. Drawing even the most obscure detail can sharpen your capacity to observe and the ability to set that observation down.

Kuhn works mornings and afternoons in a large and cluttered studio just behind his 150-year-old house. The walls are covered with pictures of animals: a few unfinished paintings can be seen alongside drawings and countless slide trays. His preferred medium is acrylic paint applied to masonite.

One of the last of the rugged individualists, Kuhn follows his own distinct artistic path. Unlike many of his contemporaries, he knows and appreciates non-figurative art, and a close examination of a Kuhn canvas reveals the abstract influence. "I absolutely love Mark Rothko," he enthuses. Other favorites are Franz Kline and Josef Albers, both thorough-going abstractionists.

In the final analysis, however, Kuhn's approach is largely intuitive. He considers wildlife art to be essentially romantic. "It evokes an experience," he says. "I do it because I like it."

FENWICK LANSDOWNE

J.F. LANSDOWNE

Raven; watercolor, 39 x 20, 1982.

"To me," says Fenwick Lansdowne, "there is something almost mystical about birds. Perhaps because they can fly and we humans cannot." He first discovered this mystery as a child when he not only could not fly, but was also, due to illness, unable to walk.

The story of how J. Fenwick Lansdowne became one of the most respected bird painters of his age began tragically soon after he was born in Hong Kong in 1937. The only son of an English electrical engineer and an accomplished amateur watercolorist and naturalist, Lansdowne contracted poliomyelitis when he was only ten months old. The disease devastated his young body and left him 75 percent paralyzed. When the war broke out, Earnest Lansdowne arranged for his wife and young son to move to Victoria, British Columbia where Fenwick was sent to a local sanitorium for crippled children for a year. He became interested in birds when, finally allowed home, he was forced to stay in bed for many months. His mother, Edith Ford Lansdowne, recalled these early years in an interview with Jo-Anne Birnie Danzker of the Vancouver Art Gallery in 1981. "He must have been about three, I think, and in a cast. One had to keep a little boy amused somehow or other, so we used to carry him off to the garden on fine days. He took a great interest in watching all the birds. He really got to know them and was very quick about it. I would go into town and buy him all kinds of bird books . . . so by the time he was four, he knew any bird by its song or its flight." His mother also got him a set of watercolors, and when she saw his first efforts, immediately recognized his abilities. Young Fenwick's interest in painting birds was diverted, however, by a perfectly natural boyish preference for pirates, cowboys and other adventurous characters. It wasn't until he was thirteen that he took a real interest in painting birds again. He was looking out the window one day, his mother recalls, when suddenly he said "Come and look at those Mergansers, Mum. They make a lovely show against that willow tree." She suggested he draw them and got him some colored pencils. "He did a few sketches and they were amazingly good. He began then, and I don't think he's stopped since."

All the while, Lansdowne had been growing increasingly mobile. A series of operations to fuse his spine when he was seven enabled him to walk for the first time on crutches, and by the time he reached ten, he was able to start the normal public school program. He was determined to become a painter of birds and spent many hours at the British Columbia Provincial Museum studying the ornithological collection. In the summers, he worked in the museum laboratory preparing specimens. The staff, realizing that Lansdowne was unusually talented and committed, not only took him on field trips, but offered expert advice on his work. Then in 1952, when he was fifteen, they organized a small showing of his paintings. It prompted the art critic of the Victoria Daily Times to write a review in which he compared the young artist to Allan Brooks, a B.C. native who was Canada's most popular bird painter during the 1930s and '40s. When he was nineteen, his mother took a portfolio of her son's

Great Blue Heron; watercolor, 38 x 42, 1975.

paintings to the high school guidance counselor, who immediatly sent it on to John A. Livingston, then the executive director of the Canadian Audubon Society. He arranged to show forty of Landsowne's paintings at the Royal Ontario Museum under the sponsorship of the Society, and this 1956 showing brought the young artist to the attention of a mass audience. The popular press picked up quickly on the new presence on the art scene, and his bird portraits were reproduced in some of Canada's largest circulation magazines including Maclean's and The Canadian. Lansdowne's New York debut at Audubon

White Crowned Sparrow; watercolor, 22 x 26, 1978.

House came in 1958. Three years later, he had his first show at London's Tryon Galleries.

In 1966, the first of seven books illustrated by Lansdowne, *Birds of the Northern Forest*, appeared in North American Bookstores. John Livingston wrote the text as he did for *Birds of the Eastern Forest, Volumes 1 and 11*. Lansdowne's first total production was *Birds of the West Coast,* published in 1976, which he also wrote. His 1977 book, *Rails of the World*, with text by S. Dillon Ripley, was prepared in conjunction with his famous exhibition of the same name organized by the Smithsonian Institute. Lansdowne's *Guide to the Behavior of Common Birds*, text by Donald W. Stokes, came out in 1978, and *Volume II of Birds of the West Coast* was published in 1980.

Usually, exhibitions of animal paintings take place in natural history museums, but in 1981, a comprehensive exhibition of Lansdowne's work was organized by the Vancouver Art Gallery, marking one of few times in recent memory when a collection of wildlife art has been shown in a public gallery in Canada.

Right from the start, Lansdowne's insistence on detail and accuracy proved to be a major factor in his work. For years, he has borrowed stuffed specimens from such respected bodies as the Smithsonian Institute, the Royal Ontario Museum and the British Columbia Provincial Museum. While working with stuffed birds helps to get accuracy in detail and size, he insists that the essence of being a good bird painter is to know what birds are like alive, and not just because a bird loses the vibrancy of its color shortly after it dies. "The better you know a bird," he says, "the more certain you are of making it into something which is true to life. You can't tell from looking at a dead bird, not even a museum specimen, how the bird appears in real life: how it stands, walks, flies away, holds its head, or even how it arranges its feathers."

Unless the idea is "so hot I can draw right onto the page with it", Lansdowne begins a painting by working through a series of rough preliminary sketches. He experiments with different compositions, placing the animal in various positions and changing the elements. Since the early 1980s, he has worked life-size because he finds it is simpler. "If you are working with specimens, you can measure them and fix things that aren't changed when the bird is stuffed. You can paint

Red Shouldered Hawk; watercolor, 22 x 30, 1975.

more easily and accurately." When the details are finally determined, Lansdowne makes a formal sketch and traces it onto watercolor paper. From start to finish, the process takes one to two months.

For Lansdowne, the bird is all. The backgrounds of his paintings usually contain nothing more than a few sparse suggestions of the environment, and, in this sense, his work can be surprisingly impressionistic. His birds, however, are rendered with extraordinary precision: his brand of high realism goes beyond what can be seen by the naked eye. Unlike many animal painters, he makes little use of photography. "Photographs are not a reliable source of information except, perhaps, for the general appearance of a bird in life, or for ideas. For one thing, the coloring is not accurate or reliable enough. Photographs can't always tell you what you need to know." He is uncomfortable letting his painted birds fly — they can be seen best, after all, when they are still — and he acknowledged this in 1981. "My birds tend to be fairly stationary. They've started perking up in the last two or three years, though, and are running around a bit more, flying more, than they used to."

In the final analysis, Lansdowne is an artist with integrity whose paintings are a record of the powers of human observation. They are born of a compulsive need to see and know. "What my paintings say, if anything, comes without my being aware of it." This may be true, but everything else about his meticulously and patiently painted works is very conscious. The subject may be birds, but the content is perception itself, and one man's need to get it all down — faithfully, and in exacting detail.

GLEN LOATES

Canada Geese; pastel, 22 x 14, 1982.

Glen Loates, one of Canada's most popular wildlife artists, says: "Rather than communicating with words, I prefer to say what I mean through my paintings."

Born in Toronto in 1945, Loates has been expressing himself this way since childhood. He first burst onto the Canadian art scene in the middle '60s while he was still a teenager, and his first exhibition, at the prestigious Royal Ontario Museum in Toronto, came when he was just twenty years old. From the start, his work has been technically accomplished and meticulously observed, sometimes achieving a decidedly Oriental delicacy.

Though he never attended art school, his technical prowess is the first thing most viewers notice. This facility developed early on. Loates remembers going to the now non-existent Riverdale Zoo in downtown Toronto as a child. Even then, he was in the habit of taking along a sketch pad and drawing the animals. Later, at home, these quick sketches would be turned into more formal portraits. Thus the pattern of work — observation, sketching, painting — was established.

When Loates was ten, the well-known Canadian landscape painter Fred Brigden came to give a talk at his school, and was impressed by the drawings Loates had taken along to show him. He invited the aspiring young artist to visit him when he had more work. Loates did this a year later, and Brigden became his teacher, quickly passing on to his student the basics of watercolors. By the time Loates was in his middle teens, he was committed to wildlife art and determined to succeed. When he turned sixteen in 1961, he was legally entitled to leave school, so he quit and went to work as an apprentice in a commercial art studio. He also began contributing to the Ontario Naturalist magazine and, in 1964, designed the publication's Christmas card. One of the recipients of that card was Gene Aliman, art director of the popular weekly, The Canadian. Aliman liked what he saw, and commissioned Loates to paint a series of bird portraits for his magazine. These appeared in the December 1965 edition of The Canadian and were such a hit that Loates was commissioned to paint another series right away.

The 1960s also coincided with a period in his life which he calls "crucially important": a period when, as an artist, he had access to the collection of animal carcasses at the Royal Ontario Museum. Between 1963 and 1966, Loates learned how living creatures are constructed as he studied anatomical structure and made drawings of fur, muscle formations, and bones. The lesson stood him in good stead. As former ROM staff artist and respected wildlife artist Terry Shortt has observed: "Very few artists possess the technical knowledge of animal anatomy necessary to portray a variety of subjects so accurately."

This accuracy is what pleases Loates most. He is what is known in the business as a "hair and feathers man." Working in his brightly lit studio, surrounded by sketches, pelts, and stuffed birds, he spends countless hours laboring over the smallest detail. With each stroke of the paintbrush, he fills in another tiny section of the surface. Standing back from a work in progress, a portrait of three goldfinches, he examines it minutely. "You can pick out every feather," he finally

announces. "That's exactly what I want. The work should be so convincing that the minute you see it, you could comment on how real it looks." While Loates' sense of accuracy is achieved through attention to detail, his sense of artistry is expressed mainly through composition and

Canada Lynx in Winter; watercolor, 24 x 17, 1983.

Bald Eagle; watercolor, 19 x 21, 1961.

Loon in Rough Water; watercolor, 9 x 11, 1985.

A good work gives a feeling of living and breathing." His insistence on seeing and studying his subjects first-hand has meant that he paints North American animals almost exclusively. A rare exception is his 1984 painting of a Siberian tiger, commissioned by the Electolux Corporation as their logo. Even then, Loates did all he could to ensure accuracy. "Going to Siberia was out of the question," he explains, "so I used my research from a previous trip to the Yukon which has a similar terrain." And wherever Loates goes, he sketches. His accumulation of drawings is big enough, he says, to last him the rest of his life. In addition, he still works from skins and specimens — a reflection of his days at the Royal Ontario Museum. His favorite subjects are predatory birds and mammals. Loates lists, as a career highlight, his painting, The Bald Eagle, which he presented to President Ronald Reagan in 1982 as an official gift from the people of Canada to the people of the United States. It was his response to Reagan's declaration that 1982 be the Year of the Eagle, in commemoration of the 200th anniversary of that mighty bird being adopted as the symbol of the United States. The watercolor, a life-sized depiction of an eagle coming in for a landing on the bough of a tree, took eight months to complete. He wanted it to look powerful but not threatening. With wings spread and talons extended, it is a splendid example of what Loates describes as "one of the supreme predators in the world at the peak moment of its grace."

color. With so many aspects of a painting already determined, the artist's main task is to arrange its various elements. Loates' approach has usually been to highlight the animal subject by reducing background detail, and in many of his works, he has eliminated the background almost entirely. There might be a branch or flower, but little else to distract the viewer's attention from the animal.

Loates third concern is that his paintings have a sense of life about them. "A painting is a two-dimensional depiction of what is seen in the wild. I try to add the third dimension.

Wildlife art is not the only interest Glen Loates has retained from his childhood. Another is cartoons. When he was young he used to make "flip-books", where a character could be made to "walk" by flipping the pages of a notepad: a process which later enabled him to study the movements of animals. He is now a devoted comic book afficianado and an avid collector of Star Wars paraphernalia. His spacious studio also serves as a display area for a massive accumulation of posters, plastic

Blue Jays; watercolor, 26 x 30, 1976.

models, Disneyanna and dinosaur models. As well as pursuing interests in deep sea life and paleontology, he is also actively involved in art and conservation projects as a speaker and contributor of works.

Loates has been a success as an artist ever since his first series of wildlife paintings for The Canadian, doing everything from designing postage stamps to illustrating books. The first book he did was *Mammals In Profile: Volume I* (1975) and *Volume II* (1976) written by Randolph L. Peterson, Curator, Department of Mammology at the Royal Ontario Museum. His works are widely accessible in limited edition reproductions, and his books, *The Art of Glen Loates, A Brush with Life,* and *Birds of North America* have made people even more familar with his work. Along the way, he has also proved that wildlife art can reach a vast and untapped audience. His work confirms the traditional view of nature as a thing of beauty: to be celebrated, not destroyed.

GEORGE McLEAN

George McLean

Great Horned Owl and Jackrabbit; casein, 1978.

In an ancient Chinese fable, an artist paints a landscape that looks so real, he walks right into it and lives forever in a world of his own creation. George McLean is not unlike that artist. He is an impassioned observer of nature who identifies so completely with his subject matter that it is easy to imagine him disappearing into one of his own paintings.

Instead, he is usually found at his 110-year-old stone farmhouse in the rolling hills near Owen Sound, Ontario, where he has lived and worked for the past seventeen years. Although he has painted exotic creatures like lions and tigers in the past, most of his current work depicts the animals and birds which visit the woods near his house. At forty-seven, McLean displays an almost childlike enthusiasm for the world of nature around him. "I've been fascinated by animals all my life. Their quality of mystery and innate ability to look after themselves intrigues me. When I see an animal I admire, I want to learn more about it, then tell the world what I've learned. For me, the best way to do that is through my art."

George McLean enjoys a life most wildlife art enthusiasts imagine a nature painter to lead. His 50-acre property includes a spring-fed pond which is frequently visited by fox, deer, raccoons, and other denizens of the woods. Every day he spends several hours observing them, and seems to have as much in common with the creatures he paints as the audience he paints for. Nature is always close at hand. Even when he works in his second-floor studio amid the amazing clutter of his trade — the big wooden drafting table that serves as an easel, the palettes, brushes and casein paints, the books, photographs and sketches, the mounted deer head and pelts of wolf and lynx — he can look onto a panorama of settings for future paintings.

It wasn't always like this. The idyllic corner of Ontario where he lives and works is a far cry from the rough-and-tumble Toronto neighborhood of Parkdale where he was born in 1939. His family was poor, and his beginnings in the tough, often violent inner city were humble and inauspicious, particularly for a would-be nature artist. Apart from visits to a local park and the city's zoo, there were few opportunities to observe animals. Few, if any of his friends shared his interest in art. Yet somehow, in his early childhood, McLean developed a burning desire to become a wildlife painter. He recalls finding a robin's nest when he was four or five, and marvelling at its perfection. In school, he showed an aptitude for drawing and spent much of his free time sketching the animals at the zoo, or copying pictures of them from books and magazines.

McLean's family moved to the Albion Hills region of southern Ontario when he was eleven, giving him the opportunity to study animals in the wild. For a budding wildlife artist, the unspoilt wilderness of rural Ontario was a paradise. A classmate taught him how to hunt and trap, and although he hated killing the animals, it was the first time in his life he was able to observe them in their natural habitat and examine the amazing textures of feather and fur. During the three years he spent in the country, McLean acquired an intimate knowledge of the animals he saw, and his skills as a painter developed rapidly.

Untitled Grouse; casein, 26 x 35, 1985.

Back in Toronto, he studied commercial art at high school and was even offered an art scholarship when he graduated. But by this time, he had set his heart on painting wildlife, so he took odd jobs and spent all his spare time drawing animals instead. "My teachers advised me not to pursue my wildlife painting because they felt it would be impossible to earn a living at it, but I had been collecting

Peregrine Falcon and Meadowlark; casein, 1970.

hunting and outdoor magazines which were filled with exciting animal art by great illustrators, so I knew there was a market for what I wanted to do."

McLean's idol was Bob Kuhn, an American magazine illustrator who later became famous as a painter of African game. After McLean wrote him several letters, Kuhn invited him to visit his studio in Connecticut, and eventually became his mentor, giving encouragement and constructive criticism. He introduced the young painter to the art directors of outdoors magazines, and for a time McLean's animal art appeared in publications such as Field and Stream and Sports Afield, but he quickly tired of the hackneyed drawings the art directors wanted and abandoned illustration.

His first break in the world of fine art came in 1963 when he acquired a patron, M.F. [Budd] Feheley, a Toronto art dealer and collector who also acted as agent for the well-known painter of birds, J. Fenwick Lansdowne. Feheley agreed to give McLean an annual salary and pay for all art supplies in exchange for his entire artistic output. The arrangement lasted for eleven years, and McLean benefited not only from the security of a regular income, but also from Feheley's tough professional advice and criticism. Says McLean today: "Budd was by far the most knowledgeable dealer I've had. I respected him because he was qualified to recognize my best work and to criticize the mediocre, but sometimes he was brutally insulting and rude. I used to watch him leaf through my drawings and casually tear up the inferior ones without comment. It was a terrible thing to do to an aspiring young artist, but in retrospect, I think his assessment of my work was right. To this day, I cherish those rare occasions when he praised one of my paintings."

McLean's work received wide exposure during these years. It was reproduced in magazines and newspapers, and his paintings were shown in both Canadian and American galleries. This led to lucrative commissions, and creative and financial

Mountain Goats on Sawback Mountain; casein, 1979.

independence. A major art book published in 1981, *Paintings From the Wild: The Art and Life of George McLean*, greatly expanded his audience, and a series of limited edition reproductions of his paintings made his imagery accessible to many collectors. During it all, McLean has remained dedicated to his art, and to the conservation of the creatures which are the wellspring of his creative inspiration.

George McLean's art seems to be realistic, but actually treads a fine line between realism and impressionism. A close examination of his work shows just enough detail to give the illusion of reality. "Slavish attention to detail of fur or feathers gives the subject a stiff, motionless

appearance," he says. "I'm more interested in interpreting an animal's gestures or its actions, and if I can accomplish this with just one brush stroke, I will."

McLean selects a gesture carefully, as the right one not only gives life and character to the subject, but also helps the viewer identify the species. To achieve intense action, McLean often devises a dramatic encounter between two animals which requires the viewer to imagine the outcome. "I'm fascinated by the drama and tension created when a predator stalks its prey," he says. "I try to portray the subtleties of each animal's behavior: to convey how a wild, free creature lives as part of its environment just as we exist as part of society."

McLean dismisses charges that some of his paintings are overly violent. "I never glorify violence or death, or make moralistic judgments in my art. The predator kills because that is its role in nature. I only tell the truth as I observe it."

Most of McLean's ideas come to him on his hikes through the bush and farmlands near his home. "It's important for me to get out every day and experience the seasons. To create atmosphere in a picture, it's essential to know how the sunlight filters through the trees as the seasons change, how the snow melts, and how the leaves grow and die." He often takes his camera along for shots of the landscape he thinks would make appropriate backdrops for a painting.

A composition begins with a series of pencil sketches which are increasingly refined and developed. Since many of McLean's paintings are inspired by certain landscapes, or objects such as tree stumps or rocks, he often draws the animal on tracing paper and then moves it over a background sketch until he arrives at a pleasing arrangement. From this he does a small sketch with all the details to be included in the final painting carefully positioned and drawn in color. This is photostated and enlarged to the size of the finished work, and then McLean redraws it on a gesso-primed Masonite panel. The painting is completed with casein watercolors. The flat matte finish of these paints gives similar textures to both subject and background so that the animal and its habitat appear to be one. The animals thus achieve a kind of camouflage, much the way they do in the wild. "A picture must have a certain overall patina," he says. "I know a painting is finished when everything looks the same."

George McLean's handling of action, color and texture has carried him to the front ranks of 20th century animal art. His work is often compared to that of Bruno Liljefors, the Swedish animal painter who died in 1939, and Léo-Paul Robert, a lesser-known Swiss bird painter who passed away sixteen years earlier. The work of both these artists is dramatic but never theatrical: creative but not contrived. They possessed a deft impressionistic touch which could capture the essence of an animal's movements or a bird's gestures in just a few strokes. McLean's admiration for these great masters indicates how he perceives his own work in the long, colorful history of animal painting. "Like Liljefors and Robert, I take an impressionistic approach to painting. But first and foremost, my work is a celebration of the beauty of nature's creatures. I try to make a statement in each painting, and unveil for the viewer some aspects of the dark, mysterious lives that animals live in the wild."

STANLEY MELTZOFF

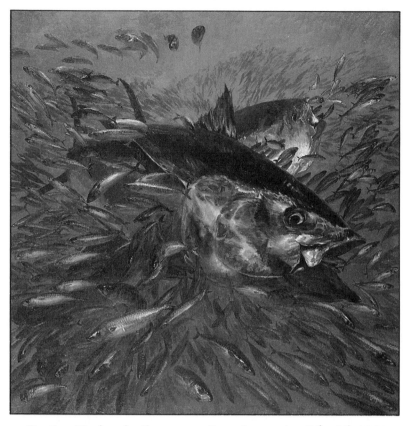

Busting Mackerel; oil over acrylic and gouache, 36 x 36, 1980.

Stanley Meltzoff is the first to admit that painting big-game fish is an odd occupation for a grown man. However, Meltzoff, a grown man to every intent and purpose, has devoted the last twenty years of his life depicting the fascinating world under water. He likes to think of himself as a magician and the comparison is apt, for he is, indeed, a master of illusion. No other painter has ever equalled his command of the liquid medium. "The trick," he says, "lies in painting the water, not just the fish." This involves reproducing light the way it looks beneath the surface: strange, fluid, refracted and everchanging.

Meltzoff's paintings are so realistic, he is often asked if he actually paints them under water. The answer is no, even though he did pose for a publicity shot in 1980 standing on the ocean floor in scuba gear, painting at an easel.

A long-time magazine illustrator, Meltzoff's paintings are familiar to millions of North Americans who have seen them in Scientific American, Fortune, Saturday Evening Post, Sports Illustrated, National Geographic, Life and other major American publications. By the time he left the field, he had won some twenty-five Society of Illustrators awards. Since the mid-1960s, he has devoted himself

Three Acrobats with Needlefish; oil over acrylic, 24 x 24, 1978.

ended with a watery encounter which lasted, perhaps, all of seven minutes. But those few minutes of relative intimacy with a creature the size and weight of a Cadillac can be a heady experience. "I'm putting into images what I see and feel," he says. "A painting is a theater in which human emotions can be played out."

Meltzoff, born in 1917 in New York City, has lived all his life in either New York or New Jersey. He studied at C.C.N.Y., the Institute of Fine Arts, New York University, and the Art Students League. Later, he taught art history and art practice at C.C.N.Y. and Pratt Institute. He has also written art criticism, and is, by any standard, expert in many aspects of the visual arts. His specialty is "visual rhetorics", the stylistic conventions in painting, and he has written a number of articles for scholarly journals on this subject over the years. His recent book is a weighty tome called *Botticelli, Signorelli, and Savonarola; Painters and theologia poetica from Boccaccio to Poliziano*. This might be a bit deep, even for fish, but any tendency to play the serious professor is offset by his irrepressible sense of humor and his aggressively down-to-earth view of the artist's role. "It's a dreadful mistake for an artist to be concerned with 'art'", he says. "I certainly don't think of my work as 'art'."

According to Meltzoff, one of the artist's jobs is to record the world as accurately and sympathetically as possible. This is particularly important in wildlife art. Although he isn't the kind of artist to worry about depicting every scale on every fish, he does go to great lengths to ensure accuracy. In his quest to gain first-hand experience, Meltzoff has gone all over the world to swim with big-game fish in their natural habitats, diving in the Gulf of St. Lawrence, the Caribbean, the South Pacific, and off both coasts of the United States. "I was lucky enough to belong to that first generation of divers who could freely explore the world beneath the water," he says. "In the forty years since I began to dive, life under the water has suffered enormously. People and fish find it

exclusively to painting big-game fish. These are not as accessible to photographers, and as he says: "The general rule is that if you can photograph a fish well, you don't have to paint it." And the rarer the game, the bigger the thrill. A diver since boyhood, Meltzoff grew up on the New Jersey coast. Even as a child, he was at home in a marine environment. He began diving seriously in his late twenties when the development of scuba equipment opened up the underwater world. "It was a revelation," he remembers. "In the beginning, the fish, who had never seen humans before, would crowd around us in the water." Then, sadly, the denizens of the deep learned to keep their distance, and as a result, finding just the right fish has become very difficult and time consuming. Meltzoff tells of a three month search for a black marlin that

Stripers at Anchor in Chesapeake Bay; oil over acrylic, 1984.

difficult to co-exist." Where there were once vast numbers and types of species, there are now considerably fewer. "The fish are disappearing . . . the waters are changing."

Although the underwater world has opened up to divers like Meltzoff, it still remains inaccessible and mysterious to the rest of us who have neither the time nor the inclination to spend months searching for billfish. The lure of adventure is there though. For some, this leads to deep sea sport fishing, and although Meltzoff killed fish himself in the early years, he doesn't anymore, nor does he see himself as a hunter. Instead, he concentrates on providing the adventure of deep sea art by observing, making mental notes, and occasionally taking pictures. Instead of inventing a scenario, he feels he does his best work when he makes a description. "If I can get the viewers to imagine they are there, then I feel I have done well. I try to put the emphasis on the total environment — what the animal looks like, how it's built, and its ambience. I want people to see how I felt when I saw the fish, and how it felt when it saw me." A measure of his skill as a technician is that when people look at his paintings, they concentrate on the fish, not how it was put on the canvas.

Seen at work in his studio near the New Jersey coast, he seems a man for whom painting is something of a struggle. "The first flush of a painting goes well, but I inevitably abandon it for awhile in despair," he says, only half joking. He describes himself as a "fast and erratic" worker. He paints standing up, the canvas sitting on a large easel splattered with various shades of blue pigment. The studio is also drenched in blue, the color of water.

In addition to slides, photographs, and his own memory, Meltzoff uses real specimens whenever they are available. Fish carcasses, some of them enormous, are hung from the ceiling just over the easel. Needless to say, they don't last too long, and may account, in part, for Meltzoff's fast and erratic pace.

A man of many interests, Meltzoff feels as comfortable in

Orca and Tuna; oil over acrylic and gouache, 34 x 24, 1973.

the 'serious' art world as he does with wildlife artists and big-game fishermen. This is unusual among animal painters, many of whom are defensive because they feel they are not considered equals by the art establishment. "It's a genre that isn't recognized by the fine art world," he admits. "If you're a wildlife artist, you're considered to be beneath contempt. That's not fair, of course." If it bothers

Eighth Ave., Asbury, Stripers in the Surf Line; sketch, 11 x 16, 1966.

Meltzoff, he doesn't let it show. He feels adamantly that 'art' shouldn't interfere with his purpose as a painter, which is to recount experience and depict the world. "Durer," he says, speaking about the great artist of the German renaissance, "never made the mistake of drawing a rabbit artistically. He just drew the rabbit." Artists, he maintains, can only do the best work they are capable of. Whether that qualifies as art is something only history can answer.

"There's still a need for artists who paint things that can't be photographed or fully seen, and for painters who describe," he says, although he also realizes that "descriptive painting is so out of fashion it has to be defended." For those who might object to a lack of creativity in this kind of painting he adds: "What could I, or anyone, possibly imagine that is any stranger than reality."

LANFORD MONROE

First Snow; oil, 18 x 24, 1983.

Lanford Monroe, with her quiet and atmospheric outdoors paintings, is causing quite a stir in the world of wildlife art. Her paintings have a soft realism in which animals fit into the canvas landscape as naturally as they would in real life. David Lank describes her as "a truly superior technical landscape artist," and even critics not entirely enamored of animal art are praising her work.

She was born in 1950 into an artistic atmosphere. "It never occurred to me that there was anything special about being an artist since everyone around me painted. I always assumed that I would be one too — it just seemed as natural as breathing." Her father, wildlife artist C.E. Monroe, and mother, portraitist Beth F. Monroe, taught her the basics. "Dad was mainly painting outdoors stuff for Collier's and Life, and I went in that direction too. But mainly they just encouraged me and never tried to impose their style on me." She felt artistic influences outside the family as well. The community of Bridgewater, Connecticut where she grew up was composed of a number of artists, and friends of the family included one of the greats in wildlife art, Bob Kuhn, and the most famous of the Western painters, John Clymer. "They've always been wonderful to me," Lanford

Monroe says. "Years later, when I went to live out west, John, who hadn't seen me since I was fourteen, introduced me around the galleries and did everything he could to help me, and I still swing round to see Bob Kuhn whenever I get up to New York."

Young Lanford Monroe not only learned painting and drawing early on, but some of the artistic facts of life as well. At the age of six, her father's manager got her a job doing a series of works for a Jenny Doll campaign, and not only was it her first commission, but also the first time she had to pay a percentage to an agent. Undeterred, she kept on learning. The works of the great Swedish wildlife painter Bruno Liljefors was an influence when she was a child, as well as the books of Earnest Thomas Seton (1860 — 1946), who also achieved fame as the founder of the American Boy Scouts. In her teens she continued to paint "influenced, like everyone else, by Wyeth," and eventually went to the Ringling School of Art in Florida. By that time, however, her naturalistic style was evolving and she had begun to specialize in watercolors. "What they were concentrating on in the early '70s was objective art. My subjective style was so different from that kind of modernistic approach that I felt I wasn't learning enough, so I left to go on my own after a year."

She was nudged further into wildlife art during four years she spent in South Dakota, and her landscape painting skills were honed doing commissions for the local ranchers. "I had a lot of respect for them," she says. "They had never had any artistic exposure and yet they were very open and enthusiastic about what I was doing. Often, they would commission me to paint some part of their land since this was what was important to them — what they loved. Sometimes I would do a painting of some particular bit of land they liked best in exchange for a heifer or for something else I needed." She also learned a good deal about animals when she went on hunts as a spotter. "I had always loved wildlife, but when you become a hunter, a predator, you learn to think like an animal. You learn where and how to see, you move more quietly, you are tuned in. Now when I look at a scene, I have no trouble imagining what animal would be there, what it would be doing, or where it would be doing it. I really think that those years out west gave me a feel for nature that I never would have experienced otherwise."

In 1979, she moved eastward again so she and daughter Charlotte could be near her parents who were now living in Huntsville, Alabama. Shortly afterward, the museum there brought in a show of American Impressionists. "I can't think of any single thing which had such an impact on me," she recalls. "I had seen pictures by impressionists before, but never whole rooms full. I nearly moved into the museum for the time the show was there." She was particularly impressed with the works of William Merritt Chase (1849 — 1916), and John Singer Sargent (1856 -1925), the greatest portrait painter of his time. "It changed my whole approach. I saw how to put the paint down; how it was possible to show everything without going into every little detail; how one stroke could paint a field that was so real you could smell the sun on it. By the end of the show, I was totally in love with art."

This set off an energetic but unfocussed period of painting when she seemed to be moving in every direction at the same time. She finally decided to concentrate on the two areas she loved most — landscape and animals. Gradually, as the landscapes became more and more important, the subjects became smaller parts of the composition until she arrived at her present style, paintings of the land with the animals in them "as I see them." This type of reality is important to her work, and she is a strong advocate of location painting, believing that it is not only good for the painting but for whatever ails you. "Whenever I feel myself tightening up, I go out painting. I find that it makes my work much fresher and bolder." She doesn't have far to go to find inspiration. Her ten-acre farm near Athens, Alabama is situated in the rolling countryside near the Elk River, and, although her work reflects her travels all around the United States, many of her best paintings, including Kingfisher Pool, Patrol,

The Fisherman; oil, 36 x 24, 1982.

Backwater — Heron, The Fisherman, and Tupelo Swamp, were done within an hour's drive of home. She is comfortable with the gentle landscape, and her creatures are not the large or fierce species popular with many other wildlife artists, but small mammals like foxes, and even ducks and geese on occasion.

Monroe uses photography to refresh her visual memory, and although she may have a vague idea before she starts a painting of how she wants it to look, she lets it develop the way it seems to want to go. While some wildlife artists have every detail worked out before the brush hits the canvas, Lanford Monroe adopts a more organic approach, and works as swiftly as possible. "The most important thing when you paint this way is knowing when to stop.

Sometimes I will finish a painting in two hours, and sometimes it will take two weeks. But if I don't feel that it is right within the first couple of days, I let it go."

These days, Lanford Monroe finds herself in the forefront of the new wildlife painters, although she prefers to be thought of just as an artist without the accompanying appellations of either 'woman' or 'wildlife', and while those in the generation before her might have chafed at the restrictions imposed on them by the magazine and publishing markets, this group has to deal with the responsibility of freedom. Even though they still have to make a living, they also have more artistic

Sunrise at Stuttgart; oil, 36 x 24, 1985.

Tupelo Swamp; oil, 36 x 24, 1982.

license to do what they want; to work on their own ideas, not those of an editor; to choose what they want to paint, not only what will sell. Lanford Monroe has found that you never get something for nothing, and that even freedom has a price. "When I have finished a painting, I never have the feeling that it is a major work. I have to learn not to be disappointed because it is not a novel of earth-shattering importance, not even a paragraph … just, perhaps, an excellent sentence. I must learn to be pleased with it, enjoy it and let go of it. But record it so that, in time, all the simple sentences can be read together and then, hopefully, become a 'major'."

However, each of the paintings Monroe considers only part of the whole seem to affect the viewer wholly. One of the reasons her work stands out is that it has broken away from the traditional wildlife art into a style which can best be described as impressionistic realism: a style which captures the feeling of a landscape in which the animals are a simple and natural part. A fox crosses the road and glances at us as it goes. There is beauty here. As an artist, Lanford Monroe communicates with us on an emotional level so that we can see things not only as they are, but the way we would like them to be.

RON PARKER

Coyote Portrait; acrylic, 9 x 12, 1985.

Slowly the bull moose raises his head from the long grasses bordering the shallow lake. Mildly curious rather than startled, he gazes at us calmly while water runs from the fodder in his mouth. In a moment he will continue feeding, but for now we have a perfect view of this monarch in his forest kingdom.

With a Ron Parker painting, we do not simply look, we become involved. We see the entire picture, not just the animal. Focusing first on the eyes, our gaze falls to the water streaming from his mouth and continues down to the grass in the foreground, then comes back to the moose, his brindled body highlighted by low-slanting rays of the early morning sun. His broad antlers, reflected faintly on the water, point to the forest and draw us into the shadowed evergreens.

While it is Parker's adept use of lines of movement which lead viewers through his paintings like this, his work never appears structured. This can be attributed to his first-hand knowledge of the creatures he paints, for Parker is an avid wildlife naturalist who spends as much time in the field as his ever-increasing workload permits. He uses a camera to record reference material rather than a sketch pad.

"Sketching often leads to interpretation," he explains. "Besides, nature is by far the best artist. We can only portray what she has already done."

Since wild animals are seldom in the right place at the right time, Parker uses imagination and a critical eye to select future sites for his paintings. He views each setting with an eye to light, shadow, and lines of movement. His imagination can often be triggered by things as varied as a weathered red cedar snag, reflections on the surface of a placid pond, or the branches of a snow-laden tree. Looking at these, he can often see a painting in his mind's eye. Eventually, on some canvas, a red-tailed hawk might perch on the snag, a few graceful geese swim across the pond, or a grey wolf patiently wait out a snow storm beneath the tree's sheltering branches. They will not look posed, however, but appear as a natural part of their surroundings.

Parker also spends time watching captive animals and birds. "I think every wildlife artist relies heavily on game farms and zoos. You can get close-up detail of hair and feather texture, particularly around the eyes, that you couldn't possibly get with a telephoto lens."

Perhaps as amazing as Parker's talent with camera and brush is the convoluted path that led to his life a wildlife artist. "Meteoric" is a term often used to describe his rapid rise to the top ranks of the field. This is apt, since he went from a total unknown to his present status in barely seven years. Surprisingly, he never considered wildlife art as a livelihood until he was thirty-six years old. Born in 1942 in Vancouver, British Columbia, Parker's artistic talent surfaced early, but his greatest interest was in sports. He was a top student, and graduated from high school in 1960 with a basketball scholarship to the University of British Columbia. After two years in the engineering program, he grew dissatisfied and left to enter a commercial art apprenticeship. A shoulder injury in 1962 prevented further participation in basketball, so he took up track and field instead. Early in 1966 he set a new record for Indoor High Jump, then later that year became the National Decathalon Champion. Two years later he broke the record for Indoor Hurdles.

Parker returned to U.B.C. on two occasions: first to major in architecture, and then to get an education degree with a science major. After graduation, he taught at a Vancouver school, and although he liked teaching, found the school system bureaucracy confining and frustrating. Soon after he tendered his resignation.

Arctic Spring — Gyrfalcon; acrylic, 28 x 22, 1984.

Winter Creek — Coyote; acrylic, 20 x 36, 1985.

During early 1977, Ron Parker attended a Fenwick Lansdowne display of original paintings, and was intrigued to find that many of Lansdowne's techniques were similar to those Parker had used as a commercial artist. He thought that it must be a marvelous way to earn a living, but it was not until a bout of influenza kept him home one time that he took out his watercolors and began experimenting. Although his first attempts at depicting birds were copies from magazine photographs, the results were satisfactory. Never hesitant when confronted with a decision, he promptly quit a recently acquired job at a Vancouver lumberyard and began painting full time.

Although a few of his works sold locally during 1978, Parker might not have made it without help from his widowed mother, Jessie. Her staunch belief in his ability was justified the following year, when his first paintings were placed with the Juliane Gallery in Toronto. Parker concentrated on vignettes until early 1980, but his goal was to become solvent enough to paint full background pieces. Bob Wood, one of his buyers, decided to invest in the artist's future, and Parker Nature Art Limited was formed. His first full background painting, completed in April of that year, sold immediately.

In 1981, now living with his new wife Maureen in the Kootenay Valley in British Columbia, Parker held his first major one-man show by renting a room at Vancouver's Hyatt Regency Hotel and inviting previous customers, friends and relatives. Twelve out of thirteen originals were sold in two hours. In December, he placed three paintings with the Beckett Gallery in Hamilton, Ontario, and later signed with a major distributor to handle his limited edition prints.

In 1982, Parker switched from the demanding and time-consuming medium of watercolors to the forgiving flexibility of acrylics. Robert Bateman, in a chance meeting, provided invaluable help in establishing various techniques, particularly the mixing of acrylics. His output of major works and miniatures increased, and the demand for prints grew steadily as his paintings became better known. Later that year he held another one-man show, this time at the Beckett Gallery. Five pieces were sold before the show opened, and the remaining eight were offered on a draw system.

In 1985, the prestigious Leigh Yawkey Woodson Art Museum of Wausau, Wisconsin, chose Parker's Wings Over Winter — Bald Eagle to be shown in their tenth annual "Birds in Art" exhibition, and Fenwick Lansdowne, the man who had inspired him, was selected as the museum's Master Artist. It was also during 1985 that the general public discovered Parker through a half-hour Profiles in Nature television documentary. Demand for his prints grew at a phenomenal rate, until entire runs were selling out before their release. Winter Creek — Coyote, for example, sold out before the prints were even signed.

Ron Parker still has goals. He continues experimenting with lighting, colors and textures, and is eager to start sculpting and casting in bronze. A one year sojourn in Ontario is planned, as are lengthy photography trips to the

Black Throated Green Warbler; acrylic, 14 x 7, 1985.

Winter Pine — Downy Woodpecker; acrylic, 11 x 14, 1985.

Arctic and B.C.'s Queen Charlotte Islands. Success exacts a toll, however, so the genial artist has had to accept the fact that gallery displays and travel now take up much of his time. Stints at the easel are often marathon events with breaks taken only to spend time with his family or take his daily two-mile run. Nevertheless, the demanding schedules are met with calm determination for he enjoys his work. If success can be measured by being paid for something you like to do, Ron Parker is, indeed, a successful man.

ROGER TORY PETERSON

Roger Tory Peterson

Ruffed Grouse; watercolor and gouache, 31 x 24, 1975.

Roger Tory Peterson has probably contributed more to the appreciation and conservation of birds than any other wildlife artist or naturalist since John James Audubon. His book, *A Field Guide to the Birds*, has been the bird watcher's bible for over half a century, and along with numerous other titles in the Peterson Field Guide Series, has opened up the wonders of the living world to millions of amateur naturalists. As well as being an artist, nature writer, photographer and filmmaker, he is an accomplished ornithologist and tireless promoter of environmental and conservationist causes. Over a long and remarkable life, he has seen many more species of birds than Audubon ever did, and is credited with identifying, painting and documenting them more concisely and thoroughly than the great 19th century naturalist could have dreamed possible.

Roger Tory Peterson could hardly have imagined the astonishing career that lay before him when, as a rebellious schoolboy growing up in Jamestown, New York, he joined a Junior Audubon Club. In the spring of 1919, when he was eleven, Peterson went on his first bird watching expedition in the woods near his school, and witnessed a sight that set the course of his life. "I saw a flicker resting on the side of a tree, exhausted from its migration flight," he recalls. "At first I thought it was dead, but when I touched it, the bird suddenly spread its wings, and in a flash was gone. My fascination with birds has never waned from the day I chanced upon that flicker. For me, birds are the embodiment of being alive. I admire their spirit, their boundless vitality, their sheer beauty, and their freedom."

Peterson soon began to list all the birds he saw. He hung bird feeders in the woods near his home and arranged his paper route around the best birding spots in town, spending his earnings on field glasses, camera and paints. Whenever he spotted a bird he hadn't seen before, he made a practice of drawing a quick sketch of it and visiting the library to consult books on bird identification. While still in his early teens, he perceived the need for a field guide that would enable amateurs to identify all the various species of birds.

Peterson dreamed of becoming a bird artist, following in the footsteps of his hero, Audubon. In 1922, at the age of thirteen, he won a Buffalo Times competition for young readers with an ink drawing of a banded purple butterfly, and three years later received recognition and encouragement from prominent ornithologists and bird painters at an American Ornithologists Union convention in New York City. Here he was introduced to one of his childhood idols, the bird painter Louis Agassiz Fuertes, and nature artist Francis Lee Jacques. Peterson was thrilled when two of his bird paintings were accepted and hung alongside the works of these famous men, who also offered him advice and encouragement. The three days he spent with them set the pattern for his developement as an artist and ornithologist.

After studying art in New York at the Art Students League and the National Academy of Design, he joined the American Ornithologists Union and became friends with Ludlow Griscom. Griscom was revered among A.O.U. members for his remarkable ability to identify birds on the wing by spotting markings and shapes, which he called "field marks". Peterson thought that by using Griscom's method, it might be possible to identify any bird by its field marks alone, and started to make notations and sketches of markings on every bird he saw. "Up until then, the only way an ornithologist could

Barn Swallow; watercolor, 14 x 14, 1973.

Wood Thrush; watercolor and gouache, 14 x 14, 1973.

Guide to the Birds, but finally, in 1934, Houghton Mifflin agreed to publish a modest first printing of 2,000 copies. It sold out in a week, and since then, after numerous reprintings, revisions and subsequent editions, has sold over six million copies.

During World War II, Peterson joined the army engineering corps and did research on the effects of DDT on wildlife. His most valuable contribution, however, was the application of his method of bird recognition to identify aircraft in flight: a method known as 'The Peterson System.' After the war, he decided to earn his living by writing and painting. In 1948 he published *Birds Over America*, followed by *How To Know the Birds*, and *Wildlife in Color*, which he both wrote and illustrated, and *Birds of Newfoundland*, in which, to his eternal embarrassment, he accidentally painted four toes on a three-toed woodpecker. The success of his field guide prompted an entire series of books based on the Peterson System of field identification, including *A Field Guide to Western Birds* and *A field Guide to Mexican Birds*.

Over a busy lifetime, Peterson has traveled far in his quest to observe one winged creature or another. He has visited more than eighty countries and made numerous trips to both polar regions. In Germany's Rhine Valley, he climbed every belfry that had a stork's nest. In the Andes, fourteen thousand feet above sea level, he rediscovered and photographed a species of flamingo thought to be extinct. In France, shortly after the war, he followed a flock of sandpipers into a mine field, oblivious to the danger until brought up short by the corpse of a cow. In Africa, he braved lion country to see bateleur eagles and, near Victoria Falls, discovered two taita falcons — birds so rare that there are just eight specimens in all the world's museums. In all, he estimates he has observed over 4,000 species and actually painted 5,000 birds, including all the ones of North America, Mexico and Europe.

He has accepted dozens of honors and awards including sixteen honorary doctorate degrees in arts, humanities and science, the Brewster medal for exemplary nature writing, and the Gold Medal of the World Wildlife Fund. In 1980 he

make a positive identification of a species in the field was to shoot it and examine the carcass. My idea was to identify each species by physical characteristics which could be seen through binoculars so the birds wouldn't be harmed."

In 1931, he completed a series of paintings of field marks for a comprehensive guide to all the birds found in eastern North America. Five publishers turned down his *Field*

was awarded the Presidential Medal of Freedom by President Carter, the highest honor bestowed on American citizens.

Long after most people retire, Peterson maintains a rigorous work and travel schedule that would tax the energies of most younger men. He spends three or four months every year globehopping to exotic locales that promise exciting new birding opportunities, and always takes his photographic equipment. In the field, he enjoys what he calls "the therapeutic effect of photography," and photographs rather than sketches the birds he sees. Though the pictures may be used to illustrate his articles and books, he takes most of them for the sheer pleasure of it. He also uses them as memory jogs for his paintings, which he does in a green-shingled studio on the grounds of his home in Old Lime, Connecticut, an early American community on the east bank of the Connecticut River. Since 1974, he has concentrated on making fully developed gallery paintings showing birds in their natural environment, a radical departure in style from the small, concise bird illustrations he has made over the years for his field guides. "I was traditionally trained as a fine artist," he says. "But the demands of my field guide work prevented me from realizing my creative potential as a painter. The many bird portraits I've done for guides were straight illustrations in which the main goal was to simplify each bird's feather patterns, and highlight the easily identifiable features of coloring. There is little or no opportunity for personal expression in this type of work. My gallery paintings, however, allow me total freedom to explore creative ideas and convey how birds relate to each other and to their environment."

No matter what kind of painting he is doing, his working methods remain the same. He begins by making pencil sketches on tissue paper, then positioning them on a background outline until he arrives at a final composition. A finished pencil sketch is then completed on a sheet of

Peregrine Falcon; watercolor and gouache, 31 x 24, 1977.

watercolor paper, illustration board, or gesso-primed Masonite.

Painting begins by building up tones in the traditional English watercolor manner. Light washes of Winsor & Newton watercolor are applied to the painting surface, followed by heavier and bolder hues as the work nears completion. Finishing touches are added with tempera or opaque watercolors and acrylic glazes to achieve special effects such as feather textures and highlights.

Baltimore Oriole; watercolor, 14 x 14, 1973.

To check the accuracy of colors and markings, Peterson frequently refers to his files of color slides and to specimens from his personal collection of 2,000 stuffed bird 'skins.' He also maintains a large file of sketches drawn from life, and written notations made in the field. These, combined with an incredibly retentive memory and vast experience as a field naturalist, enable him to create polished, literal interpretations which are a delight to both ornithologists and wildlife art enthusiasts. "A painting is a composite of the artist's past experience," he says. "I try to reveal something about the character, gestures and mannerisms of each bird I paint, based on my observations in the wild. I'm trying to free myself from the field guide type of painting. I want to paint more expansively, to explore the esthetic, visual impressions of birds in relation to their environment."

So, at the age of seventy-eight, Roger Tory Peterson is just beginning to fulfill his childhood ambition to make his mark as an artist, a goal that he deeply regrets has been sidetracked innumerable times over his long career. "There is so much I want to do," he says, "but I am determined to devote most of the next twenty years of my life to serious painting."

JOHN SCHOENHERR

Cave Dweller; oil, 30 x 40, 1983.

Canadienne; oil, 20 x 24, 1984.

When it comes to portraying bears and other big game in their natural environment, American wildlife painter John Schoenherr has few equals. With a few deft brush strokes, he unerringly captures the essence of his animal subjects, and his ability to convey how they relate to one another and to their environment delights both naturalists and art enthusiasts.

Over the past fifteen years, Schoenherr's wildlife art has been hung in prestigious institutions such as the New York Zoological Society, the Brandywine Museum, the Royal Ontario Museum, and the National Cowboy Hall of Fame.

His paintings are included in numerous corporate and private collections, as well as those of the United States Air Force, Rutgers University, the U.S. National Park Service. His work is characterized by strong compositions, superb draftmanship, and a style which is almost impressionistic. "I strive to create a certain presence in my paintings," he says. "They're not illustrations, not a literal record of something. An illustration is ephemeral, designed to be tight, slick, lacking in feeling. But a painting must have its own existence, a powerful presence. It must communicate." Schoenherr is well aware of the difference between illustration and fine art. Before taking up wildlife painting full-time in 1970, he worked as a commercial illustrator, creating hundreds of magazine covers and illustrating more than forty science fiction and children's books, including *Rascal* by Sterling North, *Dune* by Frank Herbert, and *Gentle Ben* by Walt Morey.

Born in New York City in 1935 to parents who had recently emigrated from Europe, young John grew up speaking only German, and it seemed that, even in the polyglot district of Queens, he was the only one who did. In a desperate effort to communicate, Schoenherr began to draw. By the time he was eight, he was not only spending all his spare time sketching, but was painting in watercolors. He graduated to oils when he was thirteen, and started classes at the Art Students League where he learned to make etchings and lithographs under the

famous printmaker, Will Barnet. After high school, he attended Pratt Institute in Brooklyn, studying with such well-known painters and illustrators as John Groth, Stanley Meltzoff and Fritz Eichenberg. During summer breaks, he returned to the Art Students League for painting classes with Frank Reilly, whom he describes as "an excellent illustrator who was closely associated with the old French Academy style of painting, which required that every value had to be mixed on the palette and put down in its precise location."

After graduating from Pratt in 1956 with a B.F.A., he worked briefly in a commercial art studio before striking out on his own as a freelance illustrator. Soon he was selling his work to major publications. His childhood interest in science fiction, along with his knowledge of animal anatomy, enabled him to make imaginative yet convincing

King Salmon; oil, 30 x 48, 1981.

Mountain Lion; oil, 1979.

illustrations for pulp science fiction magazines. "I was especially fond of my illustrations of aliens," he says. "I created beings that could logically exist in the environment described by the writer. They were never just human beings with antenae."

Schoenherr seldom depicts his animals in regal poses, and chooses, instead, to paint them actively involved with their environment. His paintings are much more than delineations of an animal's physical characteristics. They reveal to the viewer perceptive insights into the psyche of the subject and how it reacts in its natural habitat. He aims for what he calls "a feeling of rightness" in his paintings, and in his quest for perfection in lighting, composition, shadows and movement, will often paint an image over and over again. Once he worked on a painting of a tiger for eleven years until he arrived at something which pleased him. "My approach to painting may be summed up as simple but subtle. Instead of

recording every little detail, I try to create the illusion of fur texture or feather markings with a few brush strokes. For me, it's important that a painting have its own life — that it should look like an oil painting of an animal, not a photograph of one. The physical existence of the paint should be evident to the viewer."

Another Schoenherr trademark is the unusual shape of the canvas supports he uses. "A painting only works in a certain shape. There are just a few sizes I'm truly happy with, all longer and narrower than normal." His favorite size is 30 x 48", but for some paintings, such as Highlight, Big Horn, he chooses to paint on odd-sized remnants of canvas measuring 10 x 36". Although long horizontal shapes present enormous compositional problems, Schoenherr unfailingly manages to balance his center of interest — the animal or animals — with a strong mass of contrasting background and foreground color. These paintings, with their striking shapes, eye-catching composition, and subtle earth tones and textures, exemplify best the 'powerful presence' he manages to achieve in his most memorable images.

When he was an illustrator, Schoenherr followed a simple formula for success: he adapted his client's needs to his own vision and made the best picture he could. Today, as a wildlife artist, he is able to work with fewer constraints on his creativity. "But now," he adds, "I'm working to try and please myself. That, for me, is harder than anything else."

During this period, he moved with his wife Judy and their two children to a two storey clapboard farmhouse near Locktown, New Jersey. The dense forest and farmlands that surround this historic community have served as the backdrop for many of his paintings, as well as the setting for his children's book called *The Barn*, which he both wrote and illustrated.

Schoenherr's studio is also a barn. Located behind the house, it has been converted into several work spaces. On the main floor, numerous easels hold works in progress, each with its own paints, brushes and supplies. It looks as if a small hurricane has recently swept through the room, and only the artist who created the chaos can perceive its inherent order. "Everything in here is in a constant state of creative precommitment," he says with a wry smile. A loft contains Schoenherr's library and a fully equipped photography studio, where he carefully documents each completed painting using color film and a large format camera. He is an avid photographer, and frequently uses the pictures he has taken in the field as reference aids for new works. "They act more as an inspiration than a source of imagery to be copied," he says. "I never paint actual scenes I see or photograph. Most of the situations and backgrounds in my paintings are a product of my imagination, and have evolved as I worked on them."

He likes painting raccoons, moose, buffalo, elephants and Canada geese, and admits to a decided preference for the bigger creatures. "I like large monochromatic animals I can do with a big brush," he says. "Big mammals have a nice solid form, and, when moving, are controlled dynamic masses that I find fascinating to paint." His favorite subject is bears. He admires them because they are solitary, independent creatures: social, but not gregarious. It was during his first trip to Alaska in 1979 that he developed his great respect and affinity for them. Over a period of several weeks, he studied Kodiak bear at Katmai National Monument near Anchorage, watching and photographing the large animals as they groped for salmon in the icy waters. When he returned home, he created numerous paintings based on his first-hand observations. "To me, they represent intelligence and power, and there is something primeval in the big bears that strikes a chord." In fact Schoenherr, a bearded affable man with an infectious laugh, identifies so completely with his hairy subjects that a friend once described him as "a bear disguised as a human."

He has taken many journeys in his quest for big animal subjects including several trips to the American west. The hills, rock formations and caves he has explored there have served as background settings in many of his paintings. "During my travels in the west, I discovered my great love of stone and rock and the structure they can give to a painting. In the east the land is covered with trees, but it's rock and stone and dirt that I love to paint most." A rock climber and spelunker since he was a boy, Schoenherr's intimate knowledge of stone is communicated beautifully and effectively in his paintings, and massive rocks have become one of his trademarks. "I've always admired how the great photographer Edward Weston used monumental stones. Like Weston, I use rock formations to add impact and to simplify my compositions. Stone is eternal, tactile; it adds a certain power to a painting."

TERRY SHORTT

Tm Shortt

Blackcapped Kingfisher; ink & watercolor, 8 x 10, 1963.

Probably no bird painter alive today commands more respect in both the ornithological community and the art world than Terence Michael Shortt. He is a naturalist and watercolorist with outstanding gifts, and his contribution to wildlife art is often compared with that of the great 19th century master bird painters, John James Audubon, Archibald Thorburn and Louis Agassiz Fuertes. Still, it is only in the past ten years, since his retirement from the Royal Ontario Museum in Toronto where he worked as an artist and ornithologist for forty-six years, that Shortt has gained public recognition.

Terence Shortt, "Terry, for short", is a soft-spoken, gentle man who is reluctant to talk about himself and his many accomplishments although he enjoys recalling his adventures in the wild and journeys to exotic, untamed lands.

Born in Winnipeg, Manitoba in 1911, Shortt had an almost obsessive interest in nature and art from early childhood. His mother, a talented amateur artist who enjoyed painting flowers, taught him basic watercolor painting techniques when he was seven. Soon he began to draw and paint everything he saw in nature. His father was

Long-Eared Owl; watercolor, 11 x 12, 1961.

where he studied under L. LeMoine Fitzgerald, later a member of the famous Group of Seven painters. To pay his way through school, he illustrated women's fashions for department store catalogs, and for a time worked as a bank teller. Eventually, Shortt's knowledge of birds and his talents as a painter of wildlife landed him a job at the Royal Ontario Museum in Toronto, where he began work as a zoological assistant. His duties involved setting up and painting dioramas, life-size, three-dimensional scenes depicting the habitats of exotic animals, and assisting ornithologists in making the first complete survey of Ontario birds. The work was a labor of love, and gave him numerous opportunities to travel to remote regions of the province to collect specimens of indigenous species.

In 1938, the Canadian government invited him to take part in an expedition aboard the Hudson's Bay Company ship Nascopie, which serviced outposts in the Arctic once every summer. The government often sent naturalists and artists to make records of the areas visited, and although Shortt's primary task was to catalog and bag specimens for the museum, the trip also had a profound impact on his artistic development.

Shortt's cabin mate for the three-month voyage was Frederick Horsman Varley, another prominent member of the Group of Seven, who had been sent to document the landscape and peoples of the Arctic. They became good friends, and before long, the great artist began to coach the young ornithologist on the finer points of painting technique. "Varley's oil colors wouldn't dry in the harsh Arctic climate," Shortt recalls, "so I offered him my watercolors and paper. When he discovered my interest in art, he invited me to join him on his sketching outings, which soon became impromptu art lessons. We'd walk around on the ice and he would say, 'What do you see lad; what colors are visible as the light changes?'. He taught me how to look beyond the simple lines and form of an object, and to appreciate how daylight strikes a surface, and the colors shadows cast."

an ardent naturalist and hunter, and it was an incident on a hunting trip together when Terry was eleven which set the future direction of his life. "I saw a crow steal some eggs from a robin's nest," he recalls. "In those days crows were considered vermin, so my father told me to shoot it. But when I examined the dead bird, I was overwhelmed by its beauty. The iridescent sheen on the plumage, the symmetry of its body, and the arrangement of the feathers, made me realize that even the common crow was an incredibly complex and lovely creature." His lifelong passion for birds, and his fascination with capturing their beauty in art, began that day.

In 1926, Shortt enrolled in the Winnipeg School of Art,

Two Birds and Mouse; watercolor, 7 x 14.

On occasion, Varley would criticize Shortt's paintings by scrawling pithy comments and suggestions for improvement on the back of them. One read: "Cease trying to be a flippin' scientist, lad; world's full of 'em. Needs artists." Shortt took this advice to heart and followed it for the rest of his life.

In 1948, Shortt was appointed Chief of the Royal Ontario Museum's Department of Art and Exhibits, which gave him even more opportunities to travel and observe exotic birds. Soon he was off on field expeditions to remote corners of the world, paddling on ice floes to retrieve birds he'd shot for the museum's collection of stuffed specimens, and coating liquid latex on jungle trees to make moulds that would later be transformed into convincing recreations of animal habitats.

He led major expeditions to the jungles of India, the rainforests of Uganda, the Galapagos Islands, and the high Arctic. He also made shorter sketching and collecting visits to Thailand, Burma, Japan, Hong Kong, Hawaii, all the provinces and territories of Canada, and various Caribbean islands. By his own count, he observed more than 2,500 species of birds, almost one-third of the world's bird population. He also painted over 1,100 watercolor portraits and made several thousand pencil sketches in the field. Despite the severe circumstances under which he often worked, the paintings and sketches created on these trips are both timeless works of art and invaluable ornithological records. But Shortt maintains that the idea his paintings would one day be hung in art galleries and treasured by collectors never entered his mind. "I was, first and foremost, an old-style field man," he says. "The main purpose of my art was to record the living colors of the unfeathered parts of the birds I collected before they faded or shriveled. Since some species loose their beak color within twenty minutes of dying, I had to learn to draw, mix colors, and paint quickly and accurately."

In most cases, Shortt confined his painting in the field to "head and shoulder" portraits in which he tried to set down the unique personalities and physiognomies of individual species. "I always tried to look beyond simple

Longbilled Curlew — Saskatchewan; watercolor, 10 x 13, 1959.

markings or the arrangement of the feathers to capture gestures or subtle nuances of expression. I was especially attracted to birds with colorful or bizarre ornamentation such as crests, combs, wattles and caruncles, because they made the most interesting portrait studies.

"I seldom painted details of the bird's body or the arrangement of wing feathers unless there was some unusual feature that I wanted to document, or some subtle difference between close-related species. By restricting myself to details of the head, and the coloring of the feathers, eye, beak and talons, I was able to get enough information in a single study to make a more complete painting of the bird back in my studio."

Another hallmark of a Shortt painting is a series of sequential renderings around the portrait illustrating the bird's movements in flight or on land. These simple sketches of postures, gait or wing action, provided him with a remarkable amount of ornithological information that could later be used in more comprehensive paintings. They not only give the viewer insight into the bird's gestures and personality, but also a convincing impression of its movements as they would be seen in a slow motion film.

Shortt's portraits transcend mere scientific illustration. His precise draftsmanship and intimate knowledge of bird anatomy combined with the textural finesse of his watercolor technique, injects a spark of life into his subjects. Yet his birds never display anthropomorphic characteristics. Although he is fascinated by their many faces and personalities, he avoids giving them human traits or deliberately evoking a sentimental response from the viewer.

The wealth of bird art that Shortt accumulated in his travels hasn't gone unnoticed by nature writers and book publishers. Over his long career he illustrated a score of books about birds, among them Francis Kortright's *Ducks, Geese and Swans of North America*, Fred Bodsworth's classic *Last of the Curlews*, and John P.S. Mackenzie's *The Complete Outdoorsman's Guide to Birds of Canada and Eastern North America*. In addition, Shortt has written and illustrated two books, *Wild Birds of the Americas* and his autobiography, *Not as the Crow Flies*. Shortt's extraordinarily lifelike portraits of exotic birds have also won him international recognition and acclaim in the art world. His work graces many private collections, and has been exhibited in galleries all over the world, including the Royal Ontario Museum, Toronto; the Woodson Art Museum, Wausau, Wisconsin; World Wilderness Congress, Johannesburg; The Museum of Natural Sciences, Ottawa; The Cleveland Museum of Natural History; and Oscar and Peter Johnson Limited, London, England.

After a lifetime of work in the wild, Terry Shortt is content to spend his retirement close to home: a comfortable Tudor-style house in Toronto where he has lived with his wife Audrey for the past thirty-five years. Although his art has never brought him fame or fortune, he says his life's work has given him countless intangible rewards. "For me, the greatest joy in my life has been to get

Goshawk — Yukon; watercolor, 9 x 11, 1944.

to know these birds, to see them on their own terms, and to try to understand them. If my art has enabled others to share my passion for birds and appreciate the beauty of nature, my life has not been a waste." Measured on that scale, many would agree that it has been an outstanding success.

Robert Bateman

Royal Family — Mute Swans; acrylic, 39 x 52, 1979.
Previous page: Cougar in the Snow; oil, 36 x 48, 1978.

Queen Ann Lace and American Goldfinch; acrylic, 11 x 15, 1982.

Winter Lady — Cardinal; acrylic, 12 x 16, 1983.

Ghost of the North — Great Grey Owl; acrylic, 37 x 49, 1982.

Merganser Family in Hiding; oil, 22 x 36, 1978.

Gambel's Quail Pair; acrylic, 8 x 12, 1983.

Evening Light — White Gyrfalcon; acrylic, 36 x 48, 1981.

Claudio D'Angelo

A Flash of Wings — Great Horned Owl; oil, 18 x 36, 1986.
Previous page: Winter Wrens; oil, 22 x 18, 1984.

Gulls and Mink; oil, 20 x 32, 1985.

Bottle-Nose Dolphins; oil, 24 x 36, 1982.

Wheeling Red Tails; oil, 16 x 32, 1985.

The Drumming Log — Ruffed Grouse; oil, 20 x 30, 1984.

Wolf by the River; oil, 18 x 28, 1984.

Orca Breaching; oil, 24 x 36, 1982.

Bob Kuhn

Dall Rams at the Snow Line; acrylic, 40 x 28, 1982.
Previous page: Brer Fox; acrylic, 24 x 36, 1976.

Ice Palace; acrylic, 22 x 32, 1986.

Languid Lady; acrylic, 20 x 36, 1984.

Poached Salmon; acrylic, 24 x 36, 1974.

Rio de Oro; acrylic, 24 x 36, 1983.

Rounding Up the Strays; acrylic, 24 x 40, 1984.

Three Big Rams; acrylic, 14 x 18, 1985.

Fenwick Lansdowne

Red Billed Magpie; watercolor, 20 x 25, 1980.
Previous page: Great Horned Owl; watercolor, 24 x 30, 1975.

Snowy Owl; watercolor, 34 x 26, 1980.

Brown Pelican; watercolor, 48 x 55, 1975.

Barn Owls; watercolor, 34 x 26, 1982.

Gyrfalcon; watercolor, 38 x 41, 1982.

Greater Scaup; watercolor, 25 x 34, 1976.

Saw-Whet Owl; watercolor, 20 x 24, 1972.

Glen Loates

Wood Ducks; watercolor, 16 x 13, 1986.
Previous page: American Robin; watercolor, 14 x 18, 1985.

Goldfinch Group; watercolor, 13 x 17, 1984.

Pheasant in Apple Tree; watercolor, 15 x 20, 1985.

Siberian Tiger; watercolor, 7' x 5', 1984.

Eastern Grey Squirrels; watercolor, 11 x 14, 1984.

Scarlet Tanagers; pastel, 20 x 26, 1985.

Kingfisher; watercolor, 31 x 23, 1965.

George McLean

Cougar Reclining in a Tree; casein, 22 X 49, 1978.
Previous page:
White-Tailed Deer with Fawns; casein, 1978.

Red-Tailed Hawk Mantling; casein, 1977.

Short-Eared Owl Landing; casein, 1978.

Great Horned Owl and Eastern Grey Squirrel; casein, 33 x 29, 1983.

Marshall Woods; casein, 25 x 28, 1982.

Eastern Bluebirds and Cornflowers; casein, 37 X 20, 1977.

Red Foxes and Beech Tree; casein, 26 x 16, 1977.

Stanley Meltzoff

Double Header; oil over acrylic, 23 x 28, 1976.
Previous page:
On the Flats, Bones and Permit; oil over acrylic, 14 x 36, 1973.

On the Flats, Bones & Permit 2; oil over acrylic, 14 x 36, 1973.

Snappers, Sport, Mullet, Blackfish, Stripers at Elberon, Autumn;
oil over acrylic, 20 x 32, 1974.

Right Turn at Cay Sal; oil over acrylic and gouache, 1979.

Fort Shark; oil over acrylic, 17 x 47, 1977.

Homing into the Rookery; oil over acrylic, 34 x 24, 1975.

Baby Bones in a Conch; oil over acrylic, 14 x 11, 1972.

Lanford Monroe

Patrol; oil, 24 x 36, 1984.
Previous page: The Kingfisher's Pool; oil, 36 x 24, 1981.

Coming Rain — Blacktails; oil, 36 x 24, 1984.

Spring Creek; oil, 36 x 24, 1983.

Backwater — Heron; oil, 36 x 24, 1981.

Rock Ridge; oil, 36 x 24, 1986.

Veterans — Mule Deer; oil, 36 x 24, 1986.

All to Himself; oil, 24 x 36, 1985.

Ron Parker

Autumn Foraging — Moose; acrylic, 24 x 40, 1985.
Previous page: Robin and Cherry Blossoms; acrylic, 12 x 16, 1985.

Rail Fence — Eastern Bluebirds; acrylic, 20 x 16, 1985.

A Break in the Ice — Canada Geese; acrylic, 16 x 30, 1985.

Autumn Morning — Grizzly; acrylic, 24 x 40, 1985.

Waiting Out the Storm; acrylic, 20 x 30, 1985.

Autumn Fields — Red Fox; acrylic, 30 x 60, 1985.

Rimrock Cougar; acrylic; 24 x 34, 1985.

Roger Tory Peterson

Roadrunner; watercolor, 21 x 32, 1976.
Previous page: Bobwhite; watercolor and gouache, 31 x 25, 1975.

Snowy Owl; watercolor and gouache, 31 x 21, 1976.

Great Horned Owl; watercolor and gouache, 30 x 21, 1974.

Bluejay; watercolor and gouache, 29 x 21, 1976.

Puffins; watercolor and acrylic, 21 x 32, 1979.

Gyrfalcon; watercolor and gouache, 33 x 24, 1979.

Eastern Field Guide Plate; watercolor and gouache, 9 x 14, 1979.

John Schoenherr

Burning Off; oil, 30 x 36, 1985.
Previous page: Snowy Owl; oil, 20 x 30, 1984.

Morning Breeze; oil, 24 x 40, 1984.

Bear with Salmon; oil, 16 x 20, 1986.

Bison; acrylic, 10 x 24, 1984.

High Light — Big Horn; oil, 20 x 50, 1983.

Grizzly Bear Sketch; acrylic, 9 x 12, 1984.

Rams on Rock Ledge; oil, 20 x 24, 1986.

Nilgiri Pipit
Anthus nilghiriensis
Grass Hills, Anamallais, 4500'
Nov 1963 —

Terry Shortt

Canada Goose, watercolor, 19 x 21.
Previous page: Nilgiri Pipet — Anamallais; watercolor, 18 x 10, 1963.

Common Loon; watercolor, 19 x 21.

Peregrine Falcon — North West Territories; watercolor, 9 x 11, 1938.

African Spoonbill — Kenya; watercolor, 12 x 9, 1968.

Secretary Bird; watercolor, 9 x 7, 1968.

Snowy Owl — Ontario; watercolor, 19 x 21.

Bald Eagle; watercolor, 19 x 21.

List of Illustrations

The publishers would like to thank the artists and collectors whose cooperation made this book possible. We have made every attempt to contact the copyright holders of illustrations in this book. In any cases where we have not been successful we invite the copyright holders to contact us direct.

We would also like to acknowledge the assistance of:
The Royal Ontario Museum, Toronto
Mr. Fred King, The King Gallery, New York
The Pagurian Gallery, Toronto
The Art Gallery of Ontario, Toronto

176   Bear with Salmon, 1986
Private Collection

177   Bison, 1984
Collection of Carson Siple Gallery, Denver, Colo.

178   High Light — Big Horn, 1983
Collection of Carson Sipel Gallery, Denver, Colo.

179   Grizzly Bear Sketch, 1984
Collection of Tom Carson, USA

180   Rams on Rock Ledge, 1986
Collection of the Artist

Terry Shortt

1/186   Secretary Bird, 1968
Collection of Pagurian Gallery, Toronto

88   Blackcapped Kingfisher, 1963
Collection of Pagurian Gallery, Toronto

89   Long-Eared Owl, 1961
Collection of Pagurian Gallery, Toronto

90   Two Birds and Mouse, 1965
Collection of Pagurian Gallery, Toronto

91   Longbilled Curlew — Saskatchewan, 1959
Collection of Pagurian Gallery, Toronto

92   Goshawk — Yukon, 1944
Collection of Pagurian Gallery, Toronto

181   Nilgiri Pipet — Anamallais, 1963
Collection of Pagurian Gallery, Toronto

182   Canada Goose, 1961
Collection of Pagurian Gallery, Toronto

183   Common Loon, 1961
Collection of Pagurian Gallery, Toronto

184   Peregrine Falcon — Northwest Territories, 1938
Collection of Pagurian Gallery, Toronto

185   African Spoonbill — Kenya, 1968
Collection of Pagurian Gallery, Toronto

187   Snowy Owl — Ontario, 1961
Collection of Pagurian Gallery, Toronto

188   Bald Eagle, 1961
Collection of Pagurian Gallery, Toronto

192   Aztec Thrush — Mexico, 1946
Collection of Pagurian Gallery, Toronto

Terry Shortt, Aztec Thrush — Mexico;
ink & watercolor, 11 x 18, 1946.